GW00738312

The Story of Confucius

Written by Luo Chenglie
Translation supervisor: Alatan
Translators: Li Yonggui, Wang Xin, Pang Lixia

Foreign Languages Press   Beijing

First Edition 2004

Home Page:
http://www.flp.com.cn
E-mail Addresses:
info@flp.com.cn
sales@flp.com.cn

ISBN 7-119-03071-X

©Foreign Languages Press, Beijing, China, 2004

Published by Foreign Languages Press
24 Baiwanzhuang Road, Beijing 100037, China

Distributed by China International Book Trading Corporation
35 Chegongzhuang Xilu, Beijing 100044, China
P.O. Box 399, Beijing, China

Printed in the People's Republic of China

Portrait of Confucius

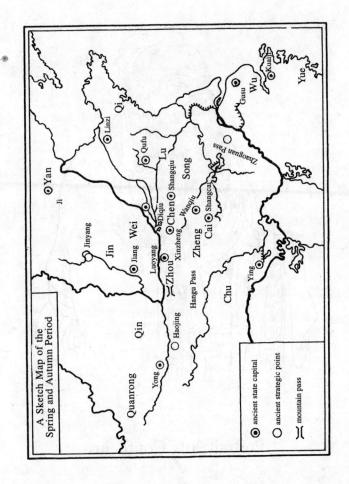

A Sketch Map of the
Spring and Autumn Period

Qi
Linzi
Qufu
Lu
Song
Shangqiu
Chen
Wangqiu
Xinzheng
Zheng
Cai
Shangcai
Zhaoguan Pass
Wu
Gusu
Kuaiji
Yue
Yan
Ji
Jin
Jinyang
Jiang
Wei
Diqiu
Luoyang
Zhou
Hangu Pass
Chu
Ying
Qin
Haojing
Yong
Quanrong

⊙ ancient state capital
○ ancient strategic point
)(mountain pass

Contents

Foreword

The Story of Confucius is a popular literary biography of Confucius, the great Chinese thinker and teacher who was born in 551 BC in the State of Lu, southeast of today's Qufu in Shandong Province. This book chronicles the life of Confucius until his death in 479 BC: His poverty in his youth, his participation in politics, his devotion to his teaching and study and compilation of classical literature, and his training of a group of talented students that helped create Confucianism, the school of thought that introduced the idea of "Benevolence" to join the "Way" of Lao Zi as one of two milestones in China's traditional philosophy that helped lay the foundation of China's traditional culture. In China's long feudal society, Confucian thought became the dominant one, and for more than 2,000 years it has been a part of the ethical awareness, spiritual life, traditions and customs for the Chinese people.

The Story of Confucius focuses on important aspects of the life of Confucius such as his family, his many travels, his life in politics, his collecting and editing of ancient books, his composing *The Spring*

1

and Autumn Annals (the first chronological history in China) and his teaching of some 3,000 elite students. While bringing to life the personal history of one of the world's most influential thinkers, this book also offers rich information about the time in which Confucius lived, the Spring and Autumn and Warring States periods (770 — 221 BC). It was a period of economic and social upheaval, but also one of the most dynamic periods of academic thinking in Chinese history when a pattern of "letting a hundred flowers blossom and a hundred schools of thought contend" in ideology created an intellectual climate of vigor and vitality.

With life-like characters based on historical fact, *The Story of Confucius* reveals Confucius and his spirit of lifelong study in a way that also can help serve as a guide to those wanting a more direct understanding of the essence of his ideology as explained in *The Analects,* the collection of the words and deed of Confucius that involves politics, economics, ethics, education, philosophy and history.

The Heir of a Well-known Father

An American scholar once said, "Confucius —
China," indicating that in the eyes of modern Westerners ancient China and Confucius are synony-
mous. Although this representation is quite inexact,
it reveals that for most Westerners their view of
China's long history, well-developed culture, civilized
politeness and harmonious surface is intimately tied
to their view of Confucius.

Confucius, the greatest philosopher in the history of ancient China, also ranks first among the top
ten great names in the cultural history of the world,
and Chinese people are very proud of the important part Confucian thought plays in the treasury of
world civilization.

In his lifetime, Confucius was but a poor scholar
who cannot be said to have achieved his political
ambitions. Nevertheless, it is this man who contributed to the treasury of human culture by founding Confucianism, analyzing ancient literatures and
teaching other famous scholars who were to follow.

According to the *Book of Confucius' Family Tree*,
the ancestor of Confucius can be traced back to

Xuanyuan, the Yellow Emperor.

The Yellow Emperor, who lived 4,000 or 5,000 years ago (when China was in the primitive society stage), was chieftain of an alliance of tribes in the Yellow River valley. It is said that he had been transformed into a human from an angel turtle, and thus he is also known as Tianyuan (Heaven Turtle). His people were so good at hunting that they were able to capture more than enough animals for food, enabling them — as the captured animals bore cubs — to begin to develop animal husbandry. That is why these people were also known as the Tribe That Has Bears. To live a better life, Lei Zu, the wife of the Yellow Emperor, is said to have taught her people to keep silkworm to make cloth. In addition, the people of the Yellow River valley also learned how to build palace buildings, boats and vehicles — all of which was attributed to the Yellow Emperor whose surname is therefore known as "Xuanyuan" ("Xuan" and "Yuan" are both parts of a vehicle). These people also are credited with later inventing primitive agriculture so that the social production at the time developed further. It is also said that they defeated in battle the Chi You Tribe from the south at Zhuolu by driving wild beasts to rush into the enemy. Shortly thereafter, they won again in a war with a nearby tribe headed by the Yan Emperor. These two wars helped form a big coalition of different tribes who came from either the Central

Plains or north and south. Later, many tribes from the east also became allied with the people of Yellow Emperor and blended in different ways. As time passed, the authority of the Yellow Emperor was consolidated in the areas of Yellow River valley and the Central Plains.

It is recorded that the Yellow Emperor had 25 sons (that is to say, there were 25 sub-tribes under the tribal coalition headed by Yellow Emperor), and had 12 surnames. Qi, the chieftain of the eastern tribes was one of his descendants. According to legend, Jian Di, Qi's mother, gave birth to Qi after eating a big black bird's egg. When Qi's throne was handed down to his fourteenth generation, his descendant Tang came to be known as a wise and able emperor. Tang "got his full power after eleven conquests" to become the founder of the Shang (also known as Yin) Dynasty after conquering the Xia Dynasty. After that, by going on several campaigns and pacifying some internal disputes, he consolidated his power, which did not fully stabilize until the reign of Tai Jia, his grandson. The Shang Dynasty lasted over 400 years (about 16th century to 11th century BC), a period of time when a slave system prevailed in Chinese history. As the most powerful slave-owners, the emperors had many slaves working for them and a great fortune in their hands.

The cruelty of the emperors as rulers in this era is exemplified by Zhou, named Shou (or Shou Xin), the last emperor of the Shang Dynasty and one of history's notorious tyrants. With most nobles in the last years of the Shang Dynasty leading a dissipated life — they seemed to be drunk or in a dream every day — Zhou was typical of them. Zhou piled burdens on his people to satisfy his increasing greed, extorting more and more tributes from his dependent states so that the people were boiling with resentment. Meanwhile, he lavished favors on Da Ji (one of his concubines) and put crafty sycophants in charge of important tasks, leading to extreme corruption. Some loyal ministers (for example, Bi Gan and Shang Rong) who tried remonstrating with him were executed by him. Others (Qi Zi, a royal relative and minister, for example) were driven to madness or were forced to flee. Even Wei Zi, the elder brother of Zhou, could not escape such a fate.

Wei Zi, named Qi, was the eldest son of Di Yi, the 30th king of the Shang Dynasty. At the time he was born, his mother was not the wife but a concubine of the king.

A few years later, Wei Zi's mother was upgraded to become the king's wife after his former wife died. She then gave birth to Zhou who became the only legal heir to the throne, not Wei Zi who failed to succeed to the power although he was Zhou's elder brother. Since Wei Zi was kind, merciful and peaceful in nature, he was determined — out of concern for the future — to speak to his younger brother about his increasing greed, arrogance, and cruelty. However, at first King Zhou just turned a deaf ear. Then he was outspoken in his dislike for Wei Zi. Still later he even warned Wei Zi not to poke his nose into his business or else. Wei Zi's efforts came to nothing, although it is evident that the effort made was not only for the good of his brother, but for the 400-year-old Shang Dynasty as well. To assure his safety, Wei Zi had to flee under an assumed name to protect himself from the insult of possible national subjugation.

During the 11th century BC, King Zhou was attacked by troops of the western Zhou led by King Wu. In a battle at Muye (the southwest part of the present-day Qi County, Henan Province), a nearby suburb of the capital of the Shang Dynasty, King Zhou burned himself to death at Lutai when his slave soldiers turned coat. The Shang Dynasty was destroyed in one blow.

At this moment, Wei Zi, as a minister of surrender, knelt down before the horse of King Wu to welcome an army of a just cause. Having long heard of Wei Zi's wisdom and loyalty, King Wu regarded him with special respect and conferred on him — together with Wu Geng, the son of King Zhou — a territory to the far east.

Soon after, however, Wu Geng ganged up with Guan Shu, Cai Shu and Huo Shu — the three high-ranking officials sent by King Wu to supervise Wu

Geng — to launch a rebellion. This was quickly put down, and the four men were beheaded. In the course of this incident, Wei Zi showed much loyalty to King Wu. As a consequence, Wei Zi was further granted the title of Lord of the State Song (present-day Shangqiu County, Henan Province) to console the adherents of the former (Yin) Dynasty. From this, it can be seen that Song was the surviving political power base of the Yin people after Wu Geng's rebellion and that Wei Zi was the founder of the State of Song.

Under the newly-established Zhou Dynasty, the State of Song became a dukedom and enjoyed much political power. When Wei Zi's son died at a young age, Wei Zi handed down the throne to his younger brother according to the succession system of the Shang Dynasty. So Wei Zhongyan became the next Lord of the State of Song, and Confucius was actually one of his descendants.

And then, after Wei Zhongyan, the fourth successor was Duke Min, and then Duke Yang, the younger brother of Duke Min, who was killed by Fu Si, the second son of Duke Min. Then Fu Si offered the throne to his elder brother, Fu Fuhe, who declined. So Fu Si ascended the throne himself as Duke Li and to his elder brother Fu Fuhe conferred Li (the present-day Xiayi, Henan Province). Esteemed for his role in abdicating the throne, Fu Fuhe is the tenth generation ancestor of Confucius.

The great grandson of Fu Fuhe was Zheng Kaofu, known for his knowledge of ancient literatures and modest and simple life. Although he assisted Duke Dai, Duke Wu and Duke Xuan in succession in governing the State, Zheng Kaofu did not claim credit for himself. It is recorded that a tripod pot (symbol of destiny) was enshrined and worshipped in his house, on which was engraved this inscription:

"Every time I accept a position, I always express my greatest sincerity, first lowering my head and then walking with stooped shoulders to take orders. When I walk in the street, I never swagger. I use this pot to cook food and take its inscription as my motto."

According to legend, Zheng Kaofu edited and catalogued some well-known literary works such as *Xuan Niao* (Black Bird) and *Yin Wu* that are now included in the "Ode to the Shang Dynasty" of *The Book of Songs*. That these odes give a vivid description of the history of the Shang people — singing the praises of the merits of the forerunners of the Shang Dynasty — offers a good indication of how much Zheng Kaofu admired and respected his ancestors. It is a fact that his way of life and his attitude had some effect on Confucius.

Kong Fujia, son of Zheng Kaofu, twice took the post of Da Si Ma, the commander-in-chief of the troops in the reign of both Duke Mu and Duke

Shang in the State of Song. However, Kong Fujia fell prey to a political struggle among the nobles. One day, his wife, one of the beauties in the State, was noticed by Hua Du, whose power was second only to the king. Hua Du started a smear campaign against Kong Fujia in order to take his wife. He spread the rumor that the poverty of his State was the result of successive military expansions and that Kong Fujia was the chief culprit behind the poverty.

Meanwhile, Kong Fujia was so honest that he did not pay much attention to these rumors, nor did he bother to give any explanation to his people. As a result, the next year Hua Du was able to kill Kong Fujia and forcibly take his wife with the help of the discontent of the people. Further when the king, Duke Yang, complained about this unfair treatment of Kong Fujia, this led to the king himself being killed by Hua Du, an event in the history of the State of Song known as "the Treachery of Hua Du." The incident reveals how powerful senior officials were at the time and how the power of Confucius' ancestors began to decline.

Hua Du was so malicious that — to leave no chance for Kong Fujia — he decided to kill the son of Kong Fujia, Mu Jinfu. However, he failed when Mu Jinfu took a chance to escape to the State of Lu. Mu Jinfu chose this State as a good place to move to for several reasons: The State of Lu (in the southwest of present-day Shandong Province) was a neighboring state and larger in area as well. In addition, Lu had always been considered the origin of Shang people. It was from here that Pan Geng, the first king of Shang people, moved to an area known as Yin (in present-day Anyang, Henan Province). So there were still some adherents of the Shang Dynasty living in Yan (in present-day Qufu, Shandong Province) at the time.

Mu Jinfu kept quiet in the State of Lu for a long time since he was there for political asylum and had lost his identity as a nobleman. It was many years later that his grandson, Kong Fangshu, took a post as governor of Fangyi, working as a private official in a private county conferred to Zang Sunshi, a noble of the State of Lu. Even the name of Kong Fangshu was due to his post (the word "fang" means "defense") in Fangyi, about 15 km away in the east from the capital city of Lu. So, great importance was attached to Kong Fangshu's taking this position because — even though the position was of low rank — it meant the resumption of the nobility of the Kong (i.e., Confucius) family.

Although the ancestors of Confucius were refugees in the State of Lu, Confucius was very proud of this, he said, because he was a "descendant of sages" such as Huang Di (Yellow Emperor), Qi, Tang and Wei Zi whose fame glows in the pages of history.

The "Sage" Born in a Cave

When Kong Fangshu, the great grandfather of Confucius, became governor of Fangyi in the State of Lu and restored his title of nobility, he certainly would have tried his best not to lose it again. Bo Xia, son of Fangshu, succeeded to his post and did his best to provide his son, Shu Liangge, with a good education.

Shu Liangge (also known as Zou Shuge or Kong Ge) was a man full of valor and heroic spirit. Tall and strong, Shu worked very hard even from his childhood in both studying ancient literature and the rites and learning martial arts. As a warrior, he not only had extraordinary muscular strength and was good at using various kinds of weapons, but he also understood very well how to fight a battle. He was brave and had a strong will. So he was appointed the governor of Zouyi, a small county 25 km away to the southeast of the capital city of the State of Lu and 5 km away to the south of Fangyi. It was a charming mountainous area, with Mount Changping in the south and Mount Niqiu in the north, both of which were densely wooded. Being the governor (similar to a sheriff) of Zouyi, Shu Liangge was in charge of both civil administration and military defense. It was not a very high ranking post, but he was the head of this area.

At that time, when an important military campaign was to be carried out by the State, all local governments were expected to follow. This being the case, Shu Liangge many times joined in punitive expedition initiated by the State. It was recorded in history that he participated in two battles in which he played an excellent role.

During the Spring and Autumn Period (770-476 BC), when wars were frequently breaking out among the states, some states would set up an alliance with others to take a joint action. The following is an example.

It was the spring of the tenth year in the reign of Duke Xiang of Lu (in 563 BC) when the State of Jin, a powerful state in the Central Plains, got together with the States of Song, Wei, Cao, Ju, Zhu, Teng, Xue, Qi and Ni, as well as Duke Xiang of Lu and Shi Zi Guang of the State of Qi, to fight the State of Wu in the south. That summer to expand its power, the State of Jin united with the States of Lu, Cao and Zhu to attack Bi Yang (a small state in present-day Zaozhuang, Shandong Province, with a surname of Yun, which once acknowledged allegiance to the State of Chu). Shu Liangge took part in this attack as a warrior. Shu Liangge, Qin Jinfu and Di Simi were ordered to assault the north gate of Bi Yang. However, they could not take the city immediately since the soldiers inside were willing to risk their lives in fighting back.

Suddenly, to the surprise of the attacking forces, the gate was slowly lifted up because the soldiers inside had designed a plot to let in some of the enemy and then annihilate them en masse. Seeing the gate go up, Qin Jinfu and Di Simi, confident of their valor, soon entered the city. When Shu Liangge arrived in his chariot to see that some of his soldiers had broken through the suspended gate, he was very suspicious about this easy victory. Just at this moment, he noticed that the gate began to descend slowly and realized the trick of his enemy. So he jumped off his chariot, threw away his dagger-axe and ran in great strides to prop up the descending gate, shouting: "Come on back, don't be fooled!" Hearing this, Qin, Di and the other soldiers realized the danger. Turning around quickly, they saw Shu Liangge propping up the gate like a stone column. They ran out of the city with much gratitude. When Yun Ban, the governor of Bi Yang, led his men to the gate, they were so astonished to see a strong man standing under the gate that their breath was all but taken away. Before they knew what was happening, Shu Liangge released the gate, jumping away as the gate fell into its seat with a loud "bang" — so loud that the earth quivered. Not daring to raise the gate again, Yun Ban and his men hurried to climb up the tower to shoot arrows. But Shu Liangge and his men had already escaped.

On their return to their campsite, both Qin and Di came up to Shu Liangge to thank him for his help, and the soldiers, too, praised him for being both brave and resourceful. This battle made Governor Shu Liangge a man of prestige.

Seven years later, i.e., the 17th year in the reign of Duke Xiang of Lu (in 556 BC), the State of Qi came to invade the northern border area of the State of Lu. The Qi troops, under the leadership of General Gao Hou, besieged the Lu troops led by General Zang Ge in Fangyi where Shu Liangge was the governor. With such a tight encirclement, Zang Ge had to ask for help. Duke of Lu sent some soldiers to try to get through to Yangguan (east of present-day Tai'an, Shandong Province). However, the soldiers stopped at Lüsong (not far from Fangyi), fearing the presence of reinforced enemy troops. Some soldiers suggested waiting; others disagreed, arguing that death would be the only result of waiting. At this moment, Shu Liangge proposed that he lead some valiant warriors to guard their master's escape, and this plan soon got approval from Zang Ge.

On receiving their orders, Shu Liangge, together with Zang Chou and Zang Gu (Zang Ge's brothers) succeeded in leading 300 warriors to protect Zang

Ge in breaking through the encirclement at nightfall. They managed to struggle through to Lüsong, the campsite of the relief troops. Then Shu Liangge returned to Fangyi to help in the resistance.

Since the commander-in-chief of Lu had escaped, the Qi troops now found it pointless to go on attacking Fangyi and so withdrew quietly. Therefore, Shu Liangge also became famous for this feat, with words of praise like: "Well-known for his valor among the States." He became a popular general in the State of Lu. In the war, Shu Liangge was so brave and dedicated that he was highly respected by the common people. When he came to his hometown, he was so welcomed by the natives that they held a big celebration party for him. However, all these rejoicings served to remind him of a source of sadness: His first wife had borne him nine daughters but no sons. In that patriarchal society, it was the general concept that only a male descendant could continue the family line. So soon he married another woman. Before long, she gave birth to a son, but one who was handicapped and — even though the boy was his own son — it would have been awkward for Shu Liangge to have a handicapped heir continue his family line. So he decided to marry another woman. All of this was not unusual for that time.

Not far from Zouyi lived an old and learned man, named Yan Xiang, who had three pretty and virtuous daughters. When Shu Liangge learned about this, he came to Yan Xiang's house to put forward his proposal. The old man had long admired the valiant and honest nature of Shu Liangge. The old man also knew that Shu Liangge was the descendant of Tang, the sage of Shang Dynasty, and that he had accomplished great things during the war. So he gave Shu Liangge a warm welcome. All his daughters also highly respected him for his good nature. However, the eldest and the second daughters were both hesitant since Shu Liangge was more than 60 years old. But Yan Zhengzai, the youngest daughter, was more than happy to marry him because she had long been worshipping him. Seeing this, Yan Xiang, the father, nodded his agreement.

When Shu Liangge got the message, he was so happy that within a short time he made her his wife. True — their ages were different, but they loved each other and they had an agreeable life, with the husband being good and honest, and the wife being virtuous and respectful.

Shortly after their marriage, Shu Liangge talked with Yan Zhengzai, his new wife, hoping that she could give birth to a son so that he could continue his family line. His wife shared the same thought. While they were holding this thought, the couple heard of a divinity staying on Mount Niqiu (also known as Mount Ni) to the east, who could not only bless the people of this area, but also could favor with sons those longed for them. Therefore, the couple often went there to pray. The Mount was only 340 meters high, with five peaks looking just like a lotus in full bloom in a distance. It was really a good scenic spot where rocks of various grotesque shapes were scattered here and there, with shade trees, all species of birds heard in the trees, flowing rivulets and streams to be seen and heard. Soon after, Yan Zhengzai became pregnant. And the couple kept returning to pray and to enjoy the beautiful sceneries as well.

As time passed by, the day of giving birth was approaching. Both Shu Liangge and Yan Zhengzai hoped they would have a son. This had been a dream of the family for a long time. So, the closer the due-date came, the more fervently they prayed. They never failed to go together to the Mount, even when she was into the ninth month of pregnancy, so as to show their sincerity to the divinity.

This was the last time when they went up the Mount to pray. They hurried climbing up, because they were so eager to have a son. But Yan Zhengzai had to walk slowly, although she had a girl servant helping her. She struggled, panting hard to the top, and had just finished her praying and was about to return when she suddenly felt a serious ache in her belly. Looking very pale, she gasped: "I'm afraid I'm having my baby soon." The moment was so pressing that Shu Liangge was drenched with sweat and eager to find a shelter. Luckily, there was a cave ahead. They entered immediately. Shu Liangge stood at the entrance trying to keep the wind from blowing in while his wife was lying in the cave suffering from birth pangs, awaiting the baby's arrival into this world. When a baby's cry was suddenly heard, Shu Liangge, though relieved a little bit, turned round and asked, "a son or a daughter?" When he heard it was a son, he became so excited that he knelt down with a flop and kowtowed and shouted: "I've got my male heir." And then he kowtowed again, expressing his thanks to the divinity for the blessings.

On their way back home, Shu Liangge kept murmuring "Mount Niqiu" and so named his son "Qiu" and styled him "Ni." Since he ranked the second in his family, he was known as "Zhong (meaning 'second' in Chinese) Ni."

So Confucius was born on August 27, 551 BC (the 21st year in the reign of King Ling of the Zhou Dynasty or the 22nd year in the reign of Duke Xiang of Lu). The cave where Confucius was born was called "Confucius' Cave," also known as "Kunling Cave," meaning in Chinese being blessed by a goddess. The legend also says that it is so called because here Yan Zhengzai performed a divine feat when she gave birth to Confucius.

A Respectable Mother

In the *Three-Character Textbook*, there is a sentence that praises Mencius' mother: "Mencius' mother carefully chose her neighbors." So Mencius' mother had always been regarded as an example of a good mother. However, in fact, Confucius' mother was also a great mother since she nurtured and educated the most learned master in the history of Chinese culture. People keep telling stories about the birth of Confucius at Mount Ni, but there is another mythical story about his mother.

In Confucius' hometown, it is still said that Confucius was born different from most people. He was said to have "seven uglinesses" on his head alone, i.e. bulging eyes, drooping eyebrows, long ears, wide nostrils, an upward-turning upper lip with exposed teeth, a big protruding forehead, and a dent on the top of his head. In one book, some 49 different features were recorded (for instance, hollow eye sockets, crescent horns…). He was also depicted as being "with Yao's forehead, Aotao's neck, Zi Chan's shoulders, but far shorter legs than Yu's." People were certainly curious about a baby in such strange shape. It was even proposed that the baby be thrown away. However, his mother brought him up with loving care. It is also said that she had shed so much blood in giving birth to Confucius that the green grass was dyed red and that ever after the grass grown there was all red, and thus called "red grass slope."

Another legend says that, after Confucius was born, no wild grass would grow there and the nearby grass would drive thistles and thorns away to protect Confucius. Even if not driven away, those thistles and thorns would have to grow downward.

Another legend says that after Confucius was born, his mother, being very much thirsty due to excessive loss of blood, was eager to find some water. Suddenly, she noticed that there was a well with clear water. Unfortunately, the well was too deep. At this, she said to herself, "How nice it would be if the well were upside down so that I could scoop up some water to drink!" She hardly had finished her utterance when the well slowly moved on a slant so that she easily could reach the water, and Mother Yan had a good drink. Later on, the well was known as "Bandao Well" (Slant Well). This well is still there today, to the east of Mount Ni, by the side of the Mother Yan's Memorial Temple, with clear water, easy to reach. The well is said to have been like this for more than two thousand years.

Another legend also says that Confucius could eat a lot after he was born, so much so that his mother's milk was not enough to feed him. One night, a hairy creature entered his house and the baby, crying in hunger, stopped crying. After a while, a tiger was seen to jump out from the house. The tiger had come to feed him.

And then: It was a hot day. Little Confucius was so hot that he was afflicted with prickly heat. Suddenly, a few hawks came in turn to hover over Confucius, flapping their wings to cool him.

Of course, these legends are not true stories. Rather, they show how Confucius has been deified as well as people's respect for Mother Yan.

Yan Zhengzai, being an honest and virtuous girl, married Shu Liangge because she admired "the descendant of a sage." After her son was born, she loved her husband even more and took care of him in every possible way. But things turned out contrary to one's wishes. The health of her husband was getting worse and worse.

As a matter of fact, Shu Liangge was nearly 70 years old at the time. He had gone into too many battles in his life, and now he felt exhausted. Now that he lived a life in peace and love, his rhythm of life had been changed from tension into easiness. All his potential illnesses broke out suddenly one by one. So, only three years after his son was born, he passed away.

When Shu Liangge peacefully closed his eyes, Confucius' mother was only in her early twenties. The foundation of this special marriage lay in Yan Zhengzai's deep respect for her husband, and his sudden death left her bereft: It was as if the columns supporting a great mansion had been torn down. She no longer knew on whom to depend. But gradually she came to understand that now her son was her only hope and that she had to continue to live on and well, if only for her son. To extricate herself from the predicament and to bring her son up in a good way, she decided to leave her home and moved to Queli in Qufu, the capital of the State of Lu.

Queli was a lane in the northwest corner in Qufu. In ancient Chinese, "Que" means "bulletin board". So Queli was a place bustling with activities. Another reason for Mother Yan's moving to Queli was that she had actually come back to her hometown. At the time, the family of Yan was a big clan. When, several hundred years later, the great historian Sima Qian composed biographies for Confucius' 77 disciples, eight of them had the surname of "Yan." Yan Hui, in particular, was the most learned and honorable, quite popular in the State of Lu. So a widow like Mother Yan had to go back to depend on her mother's family. It would be a most important reason for her to go back. There also was a rich collection of books and many scholars so that her son could learn much more and much better.

Although she worked hard as a housewife, the young widow lived a poor life in Qufu even with the help of her relatives. What she had in mind was to do her best to create a stable environment for her son to have a better education.

Mother Yan was a woman of fine breeding; her father was a learned man. At that time, according to social custom, even if a girl had a good education, she was expected to be a good wife and loving mother after marriage. Now after her husband's death, Mother Yan felt that her duty was not only to bring up her son, but also to provide him a good education. Her husband had told her that he himself was "the heir of a sage." Therefore, their son had to have inherited the noble character and the prestige of their ancestors, and he could be expected to do something to enhance further their family history. So Mother Yan knew very well that all this would be based on a good education. She took loving care not only of his everyday life but also his studies, even though life was not easy for them. She wanted her son to understand all about this little by little. First, she told Confucius not to be unworthy of the trust of his late father and the sage kings of the Yin Dynasty. Then she told him that as "the heir of a sage" he ought to achieve something great. But first, she said, he ought to learn the etiquettes and rites. According to some ancient books, when

Confucius was six years old, he would not go to the riverside or the woods for fun with his playmates, but rather practiced with his playmates the "rites." They kowtowed or made a slight bow with hands folded in front before a clay incense burner, with a straw stacked on top of it, placed on a stone table. All was made by their own hands, an activity usually practiced only by adults. Not only was this true, according to records, but Confucius did it more than just once or twice. That would be the result of his mother's kind and patient teaching. Beyond that, Mother Yan also taught him skills for living so he could support his whole family in the future and that he could go in for public office. So, under his mother's teaching, Confucius became so well known for his knowledge that many came to seek advice.

Working so hard for the benefit of her son, Mother Yan paid little attention to her own health. She lived such a frugal life that she hated to waste even a cent. As a result, she fell ill from constant overwork. She died at nearly forty years old when Confucius was only seventeen.

The custom of the time was that his mother ought to be buried with his dead father. However, his mother had never told him where his father was buried. So, Confucius got the coffin moved to a road junction. Putting on mourning clothes and kneeling down, he kept kowtowing to passers-by in an attempt to get information about where his father was buried. Before long, an elderly woman came and informed him, presumably because her son was one of those who buried Confucius' father or because she herself had been one of his neighbors. Anyway, he proceeded to bury the bones of his dead parents together at the foot of Mount Fangshan, which was later to be known as "Liang Gong Lin" ("Shu Liangge's Graveyard").

Mother Yan, who brought Confucius up under very difficult circumstance, was also his earliest teacher. It was she who sewed the seeds of culture in the mind of Confucius. Thanks to that, he became a man worshipped by later generations. So, a Mother Yan's Memorial Temple was built at the eastern foot of Mount Ni and a Mother Yan's Pool in front of the temple. The Bandao Well (Slant Well) is still there to the east of the Pool. Mount Ni and the village where she stayed were known respectively as Mount Mother Yan and Mother Yan Village to show people's respect. In later dynasties, many respectful titles were conferred on Mother Yan.

A Man Fond of Learning

Mother Yan's careful nurturing and strict teaching was not without result: Determined to make himself the best learner in the world, Confucius soaked up knowledge like a thirsty person for water. He was both fond of learning and good at learning.

When Confucius moved with his mother to Qufu, the capital of State of Lu, they found a culturally developed place with a rich collection of ancient books and literatures.

In 11th century BC, King Wu of Zhou Dynasty defeated King Zhou, the tyrant, and founded the Zhou Dynasty (about 11th century BC to 256 BC). Then King Wu started a system of enfeoffment. Dan (later known as Zhou Gong) was conferred a territory in the east known as Lu. He was a younger brother of King Wu who had helped his brother a lot in such things as defeating King Zhou, the tyrant; setting up a system of "rites and music," and pacifying two rebellions in the east. According to the rules, he could inherit the throne as the younger brother of the king, but he was content in faithfully assisting his brother and later his nephew. When his nephew (King Cheng) was a child, he acted as regent for a few years and then returned the power to King Cheng, thus assuring his fame as a loyal subject that is well accepted in China's history. That was why he was regarded with special respect by the kings of Zhou. After Zhou Gong was conferred territory later known as the State of Lu, he was told he could also enjoy more privileges than other states. He was granted full sets of musical and ritual instruments and was permitted to dress the same as the Son of Heaven (Emperor), with systems and rites the same as the imperial court. This being the case, the State of Lu became a state with the richest collection of ancient books and ritual instruments. What was more, it enjoyed a relatively more developed economy and special political power, being second only to the imperial family. So this state could be said to have provided rich soil for the development of Confucius' thoughts.

The center of the state was the city of Qufu, with a perimeter of nearly 12 km and an area of nearly 10 km². It had 12 gates in all four directions, with the imperial palace and ancestral temple as the center, in which were stored many valuable ritual and musical instruments, ancient books and file records. Usually, no ordinary people were permitted inside. However, when Confucius happened to follow somebody else to gain access, he asked questions all the way, expressing his thanks again and again to those who answered him patiently. He seemed to be very different from other young visitors in that his "hows" and "whys" were sometimes so many that he was regarded as impolite. When he later heard about such remarks, he dismissed them by saying:

"It is just a sign of being polite that when you come across something you don't know you try to understand by learning about it. Is it polite to pretend to know when you don't know? Is it polite not to raise any questions even if you don't know?"

At that time, rites and rituals were the most important thing for noblemen. One day, when Confucius was seventeen years old, shortly after his mother's death, he heard that Ji Sun Shi, the most powerful minister in the court, was going to hold a grand feast at home. Confucius thought it would be a good chance to learn the rites. He presented himself at the gate of Ji Sun Shi's house, still in his mourning apparel. But Yang Hu, a snobbish servant guard, stopped him peremptorily and said:

"Today, we host a dinner for those of status, not for you. You are not yet qualified."

Confucius responded by telling him that his father had been a senior official, and so was he. The guard said:

"I only know the officials in the city rather than those from outside, let alone you, son of an unidentified official."

These rude words were really a serious insult that hurt the young Confucius. From then on, he was determined to become a real official, a man with high social status. He told himself that the only way was to study hard.

After that, he worked even harder. He read a lot of books, asked advice from many learned scholars and took them as his teachers. He studied not only rites but music as well.

When it came to the late Spring and Autumn Period, the world had fallen into such chaos that all rites and music systems were disturbed and distorted. As the imperial family was losing its power, many official musicians had to escape to different states. If anyone wanted to learn something true, he had to go hither and thither before he found a learned scholar. When Confucius heard of a man named Chang Hong who was good at music theory, he managed to find him; when he heard of a man named Shi Xiang who was good at playing the zither, he managed to find him and learn from him.

When Confucius was learning how to play the zither from Shi Xiang, he gave his whole attention — to the smallest detail — to Shi's teaching. After Confucius managed to learn a piece in only ten days, Shi Xiang told him with approval: "You are quick enough, and you have learned it."

However, Confucius said: "But I am not familiar enough with its beat, Sir." So he studied another ten days. Shi Xiang said again at the end: "You have got the rhythm of the tune, and you have learned it."

However, Confucius said: "But I cannot understand the profound meaning of the tune yet. Please spare me some more time!"

In the following ten days, his dedication impressed his teacher very much. Shi Xiang said to him with even more approval this time: "Now you have learned it!"

However, Confucius proposed for the third time: "But this tune is so brilliant and the sentiment included in the music is so rich that I haven't fully understood it. Please give me some more time!"

Finally, another ten days later, he said to his teacher: "I have studied it again and again, and I have understood that the composer is pure in thought, noble in character and great in virtue. It is nobody but a sage like King Wen."

Hearing this, Shi Xiang applauded and agreed with him in praise: "You are quite right. This tune is just entitled 'King Wen's Virtue'!"

It is already known that Confucius sought knowledge like a thirsty person for water and was never ashamed to seek it from the common people. He once said: "It is easy to find one faithful man in ten families, but hard to find anyone like me who is so fond of learning." His hard work, his increasing knowledge and experience had well prepared him in thought for his future career.

Because of his dedication, Confucius was highly regarded by many people. When he reached age twenty, according to the rules of the time, a ceremony would be held for him. After the ceremony, he would be regarded as an adult. Being an adult, one was to marry. Many rich families would have liked to have this young gentleman as their son-in-law. However, Confucius was used to self-reliance and was unwilling to rely on the support of the rich and powerful. So he got to know a girl named Bing Guan through a friend, and he married her. She was from the State of Song, a descendant of the Yin people as well. Confucius knew from childhood that he was a descendant of Yin people. Therefore, this marriage doubled the respect he paid to his ancestors. The couple lived a harmonious life since they had many social customs in common. So a warm family life was laid as a solid foundation for his future career as well.

Loyal to His Post

With the strict teaching and careful nurturing of his mother, Confucius had grown up to be a man of knowledge. Still, he felt that he had a lot to learn, so he went around to seek more knowledge consistently from different scholars, not only learning rites and etiquettes, but also mastering many practical skills. In addition, he married at twenty. Being both eloquent and industrious, he soon became a popular young man in his hometown.

Confucius became so popular that he had attracted the attention of Ji Sun Shi, the actual power holder of the State of Lu, who was a nobleman at the time. The well-known "Rebellion of the Three Huans" in history refers to power struggles of three aristocratic families.

In early Spring and Autumn Period, Huan Gong (on the throne from 711 BC to 694 BC), the third head of the State of Lu, had four sons (respectively named Tong, Qingfu, Shuya and Jiyou). After his death, his throne was handed down to Tong, his eldest son (who was later known as Duke Zhuang of Lu). Unfortunately, this successor did not have a son with his wife, so Tong intended to hand down his throne to Ban, son of his favorite concubine. To get more support, he sought advice from Shuya, his second younger brother. Shuya, however, proposed that Qingfu, his second elder brother, should succeed — which in Shuya's own mind would enhance his own chances of taking over power. Discontented with him, Duke Zhuang of Lu came to seek help from Jiyou, his youngest brother, who agreed to his proposition right away and offered to help designate Ban as the crown prince and even to risk his life if necessary. Jiyou also suggested killing Shuya by poisoning his wine.

So it was that after the death of Duke Zhuang of Lu, Ban took over the throne with the help of Jiyou. Before long, however, Qingfu had Ban killed and then set Kai, the son of Ai Jiang, Duke Zhuang's sister-in-law, as the Duke of Lu (later known as Duke Min of Lu). After some time, Qingfu, who had an affair with Ai Jiang, became dissatisfied with the new Duke and killed him. All Qingfu's actions already had enraged many ministers and nobles. At this time, Jiyou decided to kill Qingfu in a conspiracy with Shen, the younger brother of Kai. But before they could carry out their plan, Qingfu fled to Lü, where he later committed suicide. So Jiyou supported Shen as the Duke known as Duke Xi of Lu, and Jiyou himself was granted many fiefs in Wenyang and Fei, and appointed the prime minister. Later on, to maintain stability, the new ruler granted noble titles to the offspring of Qingfu, Shuya and Jiyou, known respectively as Meng Sun Shi, Shu Sun Shi and Ji Sun Shi.

It was years later that Ji Sun Shi held power for a long time in the State of Lu. Duke Cheng of Lu, a later Duke of Lu, tried to kill Ji Wen Zi but failed. Instead, Ji Wen Zi supported the three-year-old Ji Wu as the new Duke (later known as Duke Xiang of Lu, on the throne from 572 BC to 542 BC). So Ji Wen Zi and his son Ji Wu Zi became more and more powerful — so powerful that, in the 11th year of Duke Xiang's reign (562 BC), they divided the army of Lu into three parts to be directed by the three powerful families mentioned above. They did the same with the national tax, which is known as "the Tripartite State." A great many farmlands were under the name of Ji Sun Shi, who made such excellent use of his power to expand his economical power that people came to regard their working for him as they did working for the Duke of the State.

Ji Sun Shi's practice was to divide his farmland into two parts, one being rich and the other infertile. He had some of his slaves grow crops on the richer land and had other slaves raise sheep and cattle on the infertile land and hilly land. The herdsmen working for Ji Sun Shi were of an inferior social status. They lacked motivation to improve their skills so the livestock output remained low. Ji Sun Shi was very unhappy about this. Just at this moment, Confucius was recommended to him to take over the job. So Ji Sun Shi decided to give him a try.

Confucius had been keeping at home domestic animals such as dogs or rabbits for food or fur. As in everything else to which he applied his mind, he became quite experienced in this field. Now that he was told of a position to manage both the animals and the other herdsmen, he thought it would be a job similar to the one he had at his home. But when he actually took over the job, he began to worry about the life of the herdsmen: They did not have enough to eat or wear so that they felt listless in their work, especially when they were severely lashed. Himself from a poor family, Confucius on his first day at his post got the slaves together and told them that he would not whip them or harangue them. He broke the whip on the spot. As a different way of motivating the herdsmen, Confucius applied for funds from Ji Sun Shi to have the pens rebuilt for the cattle and sheep and to improve the herdsmen's living conditions. And then, he shared with them what he had learned from his own experiences. It took only six months before the livestock fattened up and increased greatly in number, which added a lot to Ji Sun Shi's fortune.

Confucius' success at his first post brought him much credit. Ji Sun Shi was also quite happy about that and formed a favorable opinion towards Confucius.

However, the ranch issue was barely resolved when the storehouse became a problem. As Ji Sun Shi had a lot of farmland under his name — some of which had been granted by the Duke and some of which, however, had been secured by force or trickery — he collected a great amount of grain in tax every year, which was collected and stored in a storehouse. As time passed, some of the grain got moldy due to mismanagement which meant a big loss. What was worse, the storehouse manager got so confused and his work was so chaotic that he could not give a clear answer about what was going when he was questioned by Ji Sun Shi. This had been the situation quite a while when it occurred to Ji Sun Shi that Confucius could take over this job, having proved himself in his first post.

When Ji Pingzi talked to Confucius about the new appointment, Confucius was hesitant. On the one hand he was not good at accounting, and on the other hand, he thought it would be too big a duty for him to undertake. He was just going to decline when he thought better of it by considering that since everything depends upon an individual's effort — an inexperienced person could become experienced by learning step by step. Nothing in the world is too difficult for one who sets his mind upon it, he thought. So he agreed.

Holding the Letter of Appointment in his hand, Confucius came to the storehouse. He did not show it immediately to the managers there, but watched on the side how they did their work. As he saw, the sacks of grain were piled up in disorder, and the bookkeeping was also in a mess. When he finally showed the Letter of Appointment, the old manager was thrilled because he thought it was his good luck to be able to hand over to somebody else a piece of work he found so difficult and so troublesome.

So, Confucius took over the job when he was 21 years old. He began working day and night, squaring the disordered accounts on the one hand, and drawing up plans and repairing the storehouse on the other.

In addition, Confucius considered staff living conditions of great importance to the management of the storehouse. So he provided the staff with more food and clothing to increase their motivation for work. Before long, everything came back to order again, which impressed Ji Pingzi so much that he often mentioned Confucius when he talked with the Duke of Lu. And so the Duke also became very impressed by the capable young man.

As it was the case, the most important thing for a learned man was to know and to abide by the rites, the strict societal rules followed since Western Zhou Dynasty. The rites of the emperor, duke and of the senior officials should certainly be held by a man of a high rank while those of common people by a learned man. The burial rite, one of the most frequently practiced rites, included more than fifty kinds of rituals, each of which ought to be guided and arranged by a master of ceremony. Since Confucius was quite familiar with the rites, he was often invited to help as a master of ceremony.

Just when Confucius was gaining these successes one after another, his wife gave birth to a son. Confucius was very excited, just as his father had been when he was born. Confucius went immediately to pray before his parents' tomb in acknowledgement that an heir would continue the family line.

It is reported that — in accordance with local customs Confucius invited relatives and friends to dinner after his son was born. As the guests poured congratulations on him, a court official arrived. Without hesitation, Confucius hurried out to welcome him and heard the official say in a glad voice:

"The Duke of Lu has heard that you have got a son, and His Majesty has asked me to present you this golden carp to express his congratulations and best wishes for a bright future for your son."

As he said this, the official presented a golden carp on a big tray. Confucius was extremely happy to have received the carp, and he expressed a million thanks to the special envoy. And Confucius also asked the envoy to express his gratitude and his loyalty to the Duke of Lu with his pledge to devote his life to the State of Lu.

After Confucius had said goodbye to the envoy, he returned to his wife who asked him to give a name to the baby. After the envoy's arrival, Confucius ruled out all his previous ideas and named his son "Li (meaning carp)" and gave him the style name "Bo Yu (meaning carp)." And Kong Li was respected as the Second Ancestor by his later generations. He was so respected that, even many years later, carp was never served as a dish in the Kong family. And it would be referred to as "red fish" if eaten somewhere else.

Asking Dan Zi for His Suggestions for Public Office

As an important State in ancient China, the State of Lu kept frequent contact with many other states, which was then called an "official visit." As stipulated in the *Rites of Zhou*, such a visit entails many complicated rites.

Being a small but wealthy state, Lu enjoyed a favorable reputation among the states. Therefore, many states took honor in sending personages to visit Lu. In the 17th year of the reign of Zhao Gong of Lu (525 BC), Dan Zi, the king of the State of Dan — over 300 *li* (about 150 km) southeast of the state of Lu — paid an official visit to Lu, Zhao Gong received Dan Zi cordially, and at the welcoming banquet the two men shared many views on governing a state. When Shusun Zhaozi (i.e. Shusun Nuo) asked, "Your countrymen are said to be descendants of the ancient king Shao Hao Shi. Could you talk about the history of your state?"

Dan Zi then told a story about his ancestors. When Confucius, who was then 27 years of age, heard this news, he was so eager to know about these things that one night he visited Dan Zi at the place he was staying, for Confucius himself was not in a position to be permitted to be present at an official banquet. With admiration for Confucius' modesty and his love of study, Dan Zi — exhausted as he was — told him that his forefather Shao Hao Shi, named Zhi, was said to be a large bird. "We were all her descendants, so from then on all men in my state have paid great respect to birds. According to legend, my forefather was beginning to set up his state when a phoenix, the king of birds, flew there. So afterwards, all his subjects were named after birds. He named his subjects with names of birds just like Tai Hao did with names of dragon."

Phoenix, the general supervisor, was in charge of the astronomical almanac. The Black Bird Family was put in charge of the equinoxes, the vernal equinox and the autumnal equinox: Bo Zhao Shi was in charge of the solstices: the summer solstice and the winter solstice. The Green Bird Family was put in charge of the beginning of spring and of summer, the Red Bird Family in charge of the beginning of autumn and of winter. The four birds were put in charge of the eight main seasonal division points in a year. They led them to grow crops in time. As for some specific things, they were in charge of by the Five Turtledoves, Five Pheasants and Nine Retinues. Among the five turtledoves, Zhu Turtledove acted as minister of civil administration in charge of affairs of land and people; Dan Turtledove Family acted as Minister of War in charge of military affairs; Shi Turtledove Family, Minister of Works in charge of construction; Shuang Turtledove Family, Minister of Justice in charge of law and lawsuits; He Turtledove Family, Minister of Chronicles in charge of keeping a record of events. The five officials' duty was to assist people in living a happy, stable and peaceful life. Five Pheasants were in charge of handicrafts. Their duty was making and improving instruments, unifying measures, scale and volume. Nine Retinues were nine officials in charge of agriculture, and their duty was to attract farmers to agriculture instead of leaving the land uncultivated and abandoning themselves to evil ways.

Confucius listened carefully and tried to keep everything in mind. Dan Zi was deeply impressed by Confucius' devotion to knowledge so that he poured out all that he knew about his ancestors. Confucius didn't feel joyous and surprised about birds governing a state like ordinary men, but rather he learned a lot from Dan Zi's narration.

It turned out that the current almanac used in agriculture was invented by our ancient ancestors. With the almanac, they could count and keep a record of each year and month. Confucius also learned that even in remote ancient times, his ancestors had set up an effective scheme of governing the state by assigning various officials to different posts and requiring that they help each other in administrating the state. But in the Spring and Autumn Period, the whole world was in a mess, and many states could not any more be governed according to the fixed rules and regulations. Confucius thought he had read many books and had met many people, but none of them spoke in as detail as Dan Zi. Confucius thought it was because of the decline of the power of the king and the king's inability to appoint and manage officials so that knowledge of governing the state had been scattered in minority areas. As for himself, he should try his best to inherit and keep the ancient culture in troubled times. A sense of duty to save declining traditional culture inspired him greatly, and he decided to make a greater effort at it.

Well-Established in His Career at Thirty

Time flies. At thirty, for Confucius, the page of his youth had turned. Now he was already a man in the prime of life. What, then, had he been doing for thirty years? One word is enough: "Learning." To be more specific, he had been learning rites to make himself more honorable; learning skills to make his living; learning history to observe society so as to both position himself in the society and cope with personal relations. All this learning had made him ready for entering into society to help govern the state. Through learning, Confucius had long understood many things.

In an age when all was in confusion and rites were being violated, many people never hesitated to violate conventional regulations to obtain their goals. There appeared many evil things: Sons killing their father; ministers killing their masters or having the emperor under his thumb and ordering the dukes about in his name and trying to govern the people by force. Confucius then paid great attention to "benevolence," for he believed that if all men behaved with respect toward "benevolence," the nation would be stable and peaceful, allowing the people to live in harmony. Benevolence was not an abstract theory, however. It should be followed as a system or a regulation, which was actually rites. Hence, Confucius began to form his own views of ethics, society and politics based on the idea that benevolence and rites should be combined as content and form.

Through thirty years of investigation, Confucius realized that the only way to keep peace was to resume the king of Zhou's authority. The king of Zhou should have a supreme authority. He could then send order to all people. Nobles, officials and common people — all would have to be loyal to him. A good king would make a peaceful world. The king was son of heaven, different from civilians. Only with ministers obeying their king's orders and civilians obeying their governors' orders, could the state be peaceful and strong. Therefore, everybody in the state had to be loyal to their rulers. The notion of respecting the king and being loyal to the ruler was the main doctrine of Confucianism.

Through learning history, Confucius understood many historical experiences: Some people were after power and entertainment, only to fall from the top to the abyss; some people stayed on in unfavorable conditions temporarily finally to see success at the end of a long struggle. From these examples, he put forward his doctrine of the mean. To choose the best solution after investigating, analyzing and pondering became a fundamental belief behind his doctrine of the mean. Based on the above, he advocated adherence to the great principle but with appropriate flexibility. Respecting the king, being loyal to the ruler, fostering morality and acting with humanity could not be violated except for some specific reasons. Flexibility should be taken into account, that is to follow the Way and to employ power. By not using power and following the Way, a good intention might not necessarily have a good result; but only using power and not following the Way, a good intention must have a bad result. The notion of the Way and power ran through his whole life.

Confucius established the notion of the Way of man, which was in combination with the Way of Heaven. The changes of society and the ups and downs of the nobles made Confucius skeptical about the fate and the mandate of heaven, which were worshipped and respected by people. He held an opposite view: On the one hand, he advocated offering sacrifices to heaven and ancestors; on the other hand, he acknowledged that the power of man could change heaven. So he tried to reach a compromise between the Way of heaven and the Way of mandates, respecting both the Way of heaven and the Way of man. The struggle of coping with nature and society should rest heavily on man.

By thirty, Confucius had realized the above ideas.

They served as his principles of behavior in society, and they showed that Confucius had reached maturity. In the later years of his life, he said, "At fifteen I set my heart upon learning. At thirty, I planted my feet firm upon the ground and understood the basic principles of behavior. "

Confucius studied very hard so that he could adapt to society. After diligent learning and research, Confucius was superior to others in personality, morality, and abilities. Many people asked him in admiration, "How could you gain so much knowledge?" He answered, "Isn't it very strange? When I was very young, I was in a poor and humble position. All techniques were useful to me, so I studied them very hard. " When he was asked how it was that he understood so many skills, he replied that it was because he was not an official so could spare much time to learn all kinds of skills. He enjoyed a high reputation among people for his modesty and versatility. Many people eulogized him as "Kongzi." They said, "How great Confucius is. But it is a pity that such a learned man has no recognition." He didn't feel comfortable to hear such compliments. He often replied by saying modestly, "Don't boast about me so much. I am, in fact, a man of little knowledge, only of archery and harnessing a cart. Between the two, I am only good at the easier one — harnessing a cart." The more he was modest, the more he was respected.

Starting a Private School

Confucius' fame spread everywhere, and many people came to ask advice of him. So naturally they called Confucius teacher. In order to learn more, he wanted to teach his doctrine to others, and therefore, he began to recruit students and to set up private school.

In ancient China, local education, run by government, was called "Rang" and "Xu." Government was responsible for hiring teachers and determining the curriculum, so naturally it was helpful to the rulers' management and supervision. Students enrolled in school were all children of nobles. Those in a humble position were not qualified to receive education. This educational system inevitably hindered the popularization of knowledge and the development of culture. By the late years of the Spring and Autumn Period, with productivity developing and the whole society in a mess, this educational system was out of date. Confucius was the first person to set up a private school in Lu.

Confucius' teaching was mainly concerned with rites. The rites in ancient times were of two categories:

great rites and small rites. Great rites were those you had to conform to on formal occasions; small rites were the rites you were supposed to follow on informal occasions. In addition, musical instruments were also taught so as to accompany the performed rites. Confucius' teaching method was individual instruction. In the beginning, there were only a few disciples, such as Yan Lu, Zeng Dian and Zhong You.

According to the historical record, Yan Wugu — named Lu who styled himself as Jilu — was the offspring of Huangdi. After six generations, the linear descendants of Huangdi — Lu Zhong's fifth son Yan'an — first had the surname of Cao. After king Wu of Zhou overthrew the Shang Dynasty, his grandson Xia was granted an important post. After another six generations, Xia's offspring Yi Fu, styled himself as Bo Yan, was honored for his excellent merits with a fief in the south of Lu by the government. His descendants took on "Yan" as their surname. Yan Lu led a poor life although he was the offspring of senior officials. He lived in a place called "Louxiang" (humble lane). Among the disciples, Yan Lu was the first to learn rites from Confucius. Yan Lu was six years younger than Confucius, and they shared almost the same social position. Confucius found it embarrassing to recruit such a student of that age, but Yan Lu said he and Confucius' mother was of the same clan and he should call Confucius' mother Aunt Yan Zhengzai, so they were brothers. Yan Lu was simple and honest, so Confucius accepted him as a student. Later Yan Lu's son Yan Hui also came to study under Confucius.

Zeng Dian lived in the city of Nanwu, 100 *li* from Lu city. His ancestor was Qu Lie, son of Shao Kang, the king of Xia Dynasty. As Qu Lie was offered a fief in Zeng, from then on, Zeng became the surname of the descendants of Qu Lie. When Zeng Dian heard that Confucius was a learned man, he asked Confucius to be his teacher after he made arrangements for the farm work. He was a generous and unruly man. When he asked to be admitted, he was refused by Confucius because Zeng Dian, who was four years younger than Confucius, looked much older than he was. Therefore, Confucius refused to have him as a student. But Zeng Dian stayed to have lessons. He was so devoted that later he even sent his son Zeng Shen to study at the school.

As for the disciple Zhong You, there is an interesting story. Better known as Zi Lu he was a native of Bian, a dependency of Lu, so he was also regarded a native of Lu. In the ancient classics, he was called "the humble man of Bian," from which, we know he was humble and poor. As a young man, he had had rich experiences from doing many things to make a living. He was only nine years younger than Confucius. On the first day he met Confucius, he was very rude by wearing a high hat and quiver made of pig hide around his waist. Apparently he belittled Confucius because he thought a learned man was not necessarily a noble man.

"What do you like to do? " Confucius asked him.

"I like to perform the sword-dance," Zi Lu replied.

"You've misunderstood me," Confucius said, "I mean what you have learnt besides that?"

"Martial arts are the real useful things," Zi Lu said. "Do I need knowledge?"

Confucius answered: "If a king doesn't have a brave minister who can give valuable advice, he can do nothing good. Similarly, if a man doesn't have a friend who would like to give help when necessary, he cannot know about his own defects and make any progress: How to control a running fierce horse, how to handle a bow and not have it spring, how to use a thread to make a line — all these need knowledge to make things better. While those who defame others and do many bad things, sooner or later, they will be punished severely."

At this, Zi Lu was not totally satisfied, he said: "The bamboos on Mount Nan are very straight, with no need for refinement. They can be cut down and made into implements. So, is there any need to study?"

Confucius went on: "If the bamboos were processed to be equipped with arrow heads and made sharp by rubbing on a grindstone — when they were shot, they would be much better."

At this, Zi Lu was convinced. He bowed to Confucius and said, "It's my great honor to be your student." Later, the arrogant Zi Lu became a loyal disciple of Confucius.

Besides these, there were also Ran Geng, who was seven years younger than Confucius, Qidiao Kai, 10 years younger than Confucius and Min Ziqian, 15 years younger than Confucius. They came to learn from Confucius in his family.

Confucius had no patron in politics, nor did he have much money. How could he set up a school? Reputation, patience, trust of students and sincerity became his motivation. In the past, only great nobles were qualified for education. Confucius recruited students without consideration of their social status, political standing and family background. All who had the urge for improvement and decided to learn from him were able to become his students. As for the tuition, students would bring ten bundles of bacon as tuition. This was a reform to the school system.

Confucius' students came from all walks of life. Some were descendants of nobles, some were humble farmers and merchants; some were like Qin Shang who was four years younger than Confucius; some were like Gongsun Long who was 54 years younger than he was. There were even some students who had been in prison. Confucius treated them equally. Students from the states of Qi, Chen, Song, Wei, Zheng, Qin, Chu and Wu flooded to learn from him. Thus he enjoyed high prestige in many states.

Paying a Formal Visit to Lao Zi

Confucius was famous for setting up a private school, and many people knew his name. Of the three most powerful families in the State of Lu, Meng Sun's Family was the oldest. His heir Meng Xi Zi was an honest and disciplined man, who was called by Confucius "a man able to make up for mistakes." Meng Xi Zi had been sent on a diplomatic mission to the State of Chu. Because he knew few rites, he was caught in an embarrassing situation, for he could not perform properly according to the rites on the occasion of the meeting of sovereigns. Therefore he decided to learn rites, but he was too old to learn, so he placed all his hope in his sons Meng Yi Zi and Nangong Jingshu (Zhong Sunyue).

Hearing that Confucius knew the most about music and rites, Meng Xi Zi decided to send his sons to learn from him. But unfortunately, Meng Xi Zi was sick and had not long to live. Before his death, in the 24th year of the reign of Duke Zhao of Lu (518 BC), he summoned his sons to his bed and said to them:

"Our ancestors said that without knowing rites, you would be unable to assure a firm place in society. I regret that I have suffered a lot from not knowing rites. You should not repeat my error but must learn rites, know about rites so as to show the dignity of nobles. In Lu, Confucius — young as he is — knows the most about rites. His ancestor Zheng Kaofu was a real talent. Follow my words, go and learn rites from him. You have no choice but to learn rites to keep your noble titles."

On hearing these words, Meng Yi Zi and Nangong Jingshu went to pay a formal visit to Confucius with appropriate presents. Confucius was deeply impressed by their story and accepted them as his students.

This incident aroused many people's enthusiasm for learning from Confucius. As students came in large numbers, Confucius felt an urge to improve himself. The more he knew, the more he felt his knowledge was not enough, so Confucius was determined to learn from others. In Luoyi, the capital of Zhou Dynasty, there were collected many classics, files, documents and materials. By studying there, he was sure to improve himself. It was said that the director of the library, Lao Dan (Lao Zi), was a learned and accomplished man. He was erudite and well-informed, knowing the origin of rites, music and morality. If Confucius had a chance to learn from him, he would learn a lot, so he made this request to Duke Zhao with the help of Meng Sun Family. Duke Zhao of Lu gave Confucius three horse-drawing carts and some money, supported him to learn in a far place.

Luoyi was 800 *li* away in straight line from Qufu, the capital of Lu. If walked in a roundabout way, the journey covered more than one thousand *li*. It took 40 or 50 days and nights to get there by driving a cart. Hearing that Confucius was coming to learn from him from a faraway place, Lao Zi arranged for his servants to give the street a thorough cleaning and rode in a cart to pick up Confucius in person. Lao Zi was an old man while Confucius was in his thirties, so naturally, Lao Zi was superior to Confucius in experience and accomplishment. On the stone of the Wu Family Temple, today's Jiaxiang of Shandong Province is engraved eight persons, four horses and two carts. On the left in the front, a man wearing a high hat, long gown and ribbons, somewhat fat, and with no beard represents Confucius, holding a wild goose in both hands and bowing respectfully to the other. The thin man with a beard, wearing a long gown and leaning on a curved walking stick is Lao Zi. Behind Confucius, a cart with the engraving, "For Confucius." Three men holding books for Confucius to read were workers of the national library.

Confucius learned much from Lao Zi. When he left Luoyi, Lao Zi said to him, "I heard that rich man will send money as presents and that a man with morality sends a few words. I am not rich, so as a seemingly moral man, I'd like to give you a few words. You learned from the ancients. It's a good idea. But do not restrict yourself to it or act on it rigidly. Those who are in business do not always display their excellent goods. Similarly a learned man does not always show off before others. Don't discuss others' evil. Pay attention not to be arrogant and overdo anything. Don't be obstinate and swollen with arrogance."

In Luoyi, Confucius visited Duke Li Temple, Duke Mu Temple, the Temple of Heaven and examined the construction of the ancestral temple where he had seen many ancient relics. By reading the documents under Lao Zi's collection, he enriched himself in knowledge. He sang high praises for Lao Zi after he returned, saying, "I know birds can fly but they may be shot dead; I know fish can swim, but they may be snared; I know beasts can walk, but they may fall into a trap. Only one thing cannot be controlled: It can go in the wind and clouds as it wishes. It can also go into the sky. This is the dragon in legends. I could not really figure out Lao Zi. He is more like a dragon."

A Disturbance at a Cockfight

In Lu, monopolizing power had become a big problem for a long time. As early as the 15th year in the reign of Duke Xuan of Lu (594 BC), the policy of levying revenues according to *mu* was enforced, as was put forward when Ji Wenzi was in power. And after the Three Families came onto the stage, the Ji Family became much stronger. In the 5th year of Duke Zhao of Lu (537 BC), the Middle Army was eradicated, and the national army was separated into four parts: Mengsun and Shusun were in charge of one each, while Ji Sun Shi took over two armies, as in the so-called "Four Division of the Power." Ji Sun Shi stipulated that anyone who could pay a certain amount of money could be exempted from being recruited into the army. As a matter of fact, the money was seized firmly by Ji Sun Shi. As Ji Sun Shi controlled the finance on which the country depended — the Duke of Lu, in fact, had already lost his power. Ji Sun Shi became so arrogant and imperious that he even looked down upon the king of Lu. The incident of the "sacrificial dance" was an example of his arrogance.

Earlier, aristocrats had set strict rules for rituals and music that permitted only the Son of Heaven to enjoy the privilege of offering a sacrifice to Heaven, Earth and to the altars of the gods of earth and grain. During the sacrificial ceremony, sacrifices of ox, sheep and pig were called "Tailao" (Imperial Sacrifice). Sixty-four dancers performed in eight rows with eight dancers in each row, so the dance was called "Eight-row Dance." According to the rule, dukes were only allowed to adopt "Six-row Dance." A senior official like Ji Sun Shi was only allowed "Four-row Dance." But once Duke Zhao of Lu canceled a sacrificial ceremony at the last moment. Ji Pingzi gathered the dance teams of the Duke of Lu and the Three Families to perform "Eight-row Dance" in his private courtyard. It was, according to the rules, an open defiance of the royal court and rituals. What's more, the Three Families used the Yun Song during the removal of the sacrificial vessels, which was the right only of the Son of Heaven. At this, Confucius said with emotion, "If this can be endured, what else cannot be endured!"

Ji Shi also wanted to make offerings on Mount Tai, as was also against the rituals, for only the king of Zhou had the right. Dukes were supposed to make offerings on their own hills, senior officials on their earth mounds. At this, Confucius was so enraged that he said, "I'm sure the deity of Mount Tai will see through the ritual violators and mete out punishment."

The Three Families and Ji Sun Shi's behavior was in conflict with the King of Lu and — especially after the gamecock incident — this conflict became even more intense.

At that time, aristocrats often amused themselves with cockfighting, breeding ferocious roosters and letting them fight against each other. The winner's owner won the contest. As the owners often made a bet, this was literally gambling. For each contest, a large crowd gathered to watch. And, naturally, the winner was cheered with the winning of money while the loser was left depressed. Both the winner and the loser were very nervous during the match.

Now the contest between Ji Pingzi and Hou Zhaobo began, and they each scrutinized the adversary's rooster. Suddenly, Hou Zhaobo found on the wing of Ji Pingzi's bird some mustard spread to blunt pecking. To Ji's surprise, he found Hou had put an iron hook around his rooster's claws to scratch off his adversary's flesh. Both men had violated the rules, but each insisted what he had done was right and found fault with the other.

Duke Zhao of Lu had been intending to subdue Ji Pingzi, so he and others naturally stood on the side of Hou Zhaobo and censured Ji Pingzi. On such an occasion, shrewd Ji Pingzi had to hide his real intentions. He pretended to make a compromise with Hou Zhaobo by admitting fault. Ji Pingzi declared that he wanted to make up for what he had done and asked to be allowed to repent for his error in a faraway place. But his compromise did not lift him out of trouble, because Hou Zhaobo would not accept his terms. This was enough reason for Ji Pingzi to make his counterattack. He publicized Hou Zhaobo's tricks and told the crowd how his good intentions for resolving the dispute were refused. In this way, Ji Pingzi took a dominant position in politics, and later he united Meng Shi and Sun Shi in overwhelming Hou Zhaobo and the king of Lu's attack. Finally he killed Hou Zhaobo. Soon after, Duke Zhao of Lu had to flee to Qi with his followers.

That a senior official should drive away a king! Confucius regarded this act as an open violation of the rituals of Zhou. To avoid the company of the rebellious subjects, Confucius was determined to leave the State of Lu, an unlawful place, for the State of Qi, to follow the Duke Zhao of Lu.

Discussing Politics on Mount Tai

The act of Ji Pingzi's driving the Duke of Lu out of the state was nothing but a bold violation of the rites. Confucius left Lu in anger. Therefore, it was political purpose that motivated his leaving for the State of Qi. On his way, Confucius kept thinking about — given the circumstances of great chaos and of the breaking-down of formality — how to adhere to the rites, govern the nation through virtue, advocate humanity, save the nation and restore the customs. He kept talking about these problems to his students.

One morning, when passing Mount Tai on the east side on their way to Qi, Confucius and his disciples suddenly heard a woman crying. The heart-breaking cry touched him, and he asked Zi Lu to see what had happened.

Zi Lu walked over and found an old woman crying beside a fresh grave. Zi Lu asked, "Could you tell me, Madam, who has passed away in your family?"

The old woman answered him in sorrow that it was her son. She then continued her story by saying that her family had sustained themselves for three generations by clearing the wilderness, but unfortunately, she said:

"When he was tilling the land, my father-in-law was eaten by a fierce tiger that came down from the mountain. The same thing happened to my husband. And now my son has been killed."

Pointing at the three graves, she wept so hard that no one could ease her broken heart. But Zi Lu was curious and asked: "Since there are tigers here, why don't you move away?" The old woman said, "Because there is no heavy tax for us living in deep mountains."

The old woman's story shocked Confucius. He recently had been musing over just these things: The rulers, to satisfy their own insatiable desires, extorted taxes and levies to exploit ordinary people, sucking their lifeblood so that they could no longer survive. Therefore, they rose up to revolt against the government. But the oppression and intense resistance made the nation unstable. How to end the conflict to restore the peace to the nation? Confucius had put forward the notion of "benevolence" from an early time. And what happened at the foot of Mount Tai strengthened his idea to carry on the notion of "benevolence."

The more disordered a society became, the more nostalgic Confucius became about the prosperity in the early years of the Western Zhou Dynasty. Confucius thought that the systems and politics in the early years of Western Zhou were very good and that the emperor of Zhou was supposed to be the king of the world. Only under his leadership could the nation be unified. The throne must be inherited according to the regulations and not passed on randomly. All the subsidiary states governed by dukes must submit to the "Son of Heaven" (emperor) and the hierarchy and status, too, should not be changed. The reason laws and institution were good in the early years of Zhou was that they were based on a government of virtue. A governor should not unify the whole nation with an iron hand but with mild and acceptable means. This is the concept of "benevolence."

In Confucius' lifetime, he often referred to "benevolence," i.e. carrying on benevolence in economy and politics, opposing cruel exploitation and domination. He also regarded benevolence as a moral standard and used it to adjust relations between men. To Confucius, benevolence is the supreme state of morality and the behavioral norm of one's conduct in society. A person with benevolence, in Confucius' mind, possesses lofty character and morality. Benevolence is regarded as the criterion with which we can tell a gentleman from a small man (a vile character), virtue from insensitivity, good from evil, right from wrong and truth from falsehood. If emperors abide by benevolence, the world is peaceful; if officials obey benevolence, they will do everything possible to serve and do good for common people; if ordinary men are of this moral character, the nation will prosper and become a land of ceremony and propriety.

Confucius explains that the act of restraining oneself and conforming to the rites is benevolence, that is to say, man should overcome his own shortcomings and restrain himself, to behave in accordance with the accepted norms of the Zhou Dynasty. If so, the whole world would become peaceful and everyone has his faith in benevolence. In Chinese, benevolence covers a wide range of concepts such as humility, courage, love of knowledge, conforming to formality and putting oneself in the place of another, to mention just a few. Confucius thinks that a man of benevolence should love all men and put himself in the place of another. He also asserts that "A man of benevolence should not do to others what he would not want done to himself," and that a person should not interfere with others' dignity and encroach upon others' interest. Only by treating common people in a benevolent manner can rulers enjoy long-lasting benefits. The concept of benevolence also embraces the notion that rulers should respect, unite, cooperate among themselves and safeguard the nation's security and protect their own interests. In a word, Confucius not only sticks to the rites passed down from the early years of the

Western Zhou Dynasty but also hopes to realize his goal through gentle governance and gradually reform the nation. In accordance with the standard of implementing a policy of benevolence and resuming the rites, Confucius praised some ancient sage emperors and prime ministers. For example, he once talked about the three ancient emperors. Emperor Yao's morality was as great as the Heaven; Emperor Shun appointed officials of virtue rather than those with common talents. Though Shun was respected as the son of Heaven, possessed a magnitude of wealth, he never did anything out of his own personal interests; Emperor Yu lived a poor life and labored by himself. He curbed the flood and did many good things for people; King Wen of the Zhou Dynasty was a man with noble mind; King Wu sent armed forces to suppress and killed Zhou, the notorious tyrant of the Shang Dynasty, and by doing so attained immortal fame. Confucius highly respected those who applied the policy of benevolence, as is exemplified by his admiration for Zi Chan in the State of Zheng.

Confucius praises Zi Chan for his bestowing favor to the people and his paying much attention to reality rather than in believing in spirits and demons. He admired Zi Chan's tactics of governing slaves with the policy of alternating leniency with severity. Some slaves in the state of Zheng rose in rebellion in the thick reeds at Huanfu but were put down by the army of Tai Shu, the senior officer. On hearing the news, Confucius said it was good: If governed with soft tactics, people will become sluggish, so they should be ruled by hard means. To govern the nation with hard and soft tactics in turn, the nation will be stable and peaceful. Using soft tactics makes up for the hard ones and using hard tactics helps the soft ones so that government affairs become much better.

Duke Jing Asks Advice from Confucius

In 517 BC, Confucius arrived at the State of Qi (northeast of present-day Shandong Province).

The State of Qi had been the fief of Jiang Shang in the early years of Western Zhou. It was located in the middle and eastern part of Shandong Peninsula where there were fertile land, highly-developed farming and handicraft industry. What's more, since it was near the sea, Qi was rich in fish and salt. In the early years of the Spring and Autumn Period, Duke Huan succeeded to the throne. Thanks to his appointing Guan Zhong, a great statesman as prime minister, the State of Qi came to dominate the other states while Duke Huan himself became the most famous feudal lord. Although the State of Qi declined a bit after Duke Huan died, it remained the main power and a threat to the State of Lu. At that time, Duke Jing was the emperor of Qi. To oppose Ji Sun Shi who had the real power in the State of Lu, Duke Jing allowed Duke Zhao to take refuge in Qi. As a man who always showed great respect and loyalty to kind rulers, Confucius had held Duke

Zhao's kindness in mind. He was angry at Duke Zhao's being driven out and Ji Pingzi's interfering with the national affairs by wearing Fanyu, a gem and symbol of monarchial power, which Confucius considered not the behavior of a noble man. Therefore, he led his disciples to head for Qi by climbing Mount Tai, and before long they arrived at Qi where Confucius planned to meet Duke Jing.

According to the record, five years before that year, Duke Jing had met Confucius when he came to Lu. He once asked Confucius, "How could such a backward and small state as Qin dominate among other states, especially in the period of Duke Mu?" Confucius answered, "Small as it is, Qin has high aspirations and remote as it is, its people are engaged in a just cause. As for why Duke Mu took to power, it is because he knew how to make good appointments."

Confucius gave as an example Duke Mu's taking a fancy to Bai Li Xi, a servant assigned to feeding cows. Duke Mu bought him for five pieces of sheepskin and talked with Bai Li Xi for three days. Duke Mu adopted Bai Li Xi's advice and appointed him to an important task.

"What Duke Mu did helped make Qin a prosperous, strong, and leading state at that time, not to mention dominating other states!"

Duke Jing agreed with Confucius' remarks.

This time, as soon as Confucius set his foot on

the earth of Qi, he thought that if Duke Jing trusted him, he could fulfill his ambition and accomplish his cause like Bai Li Xi.

Unfortunately, after so many years, Duke Jing had already forgotten Confucius' statements. In addition, it proved difficult for Confucius to meet him. So finally Confucius got in touch with Gao Zhaozi, a close follower of Duke Jing who agreed to send his regards to the Duke. With Gao Zhaozi's help, Duke Jing condescended as an emperor of a state to meet Confucius, who was still an unsuccessful "shi" (a social stratum in ancient China, between senior officials and the common people.)

"What shall we do to run the nation?" Duke Jing asked Confucius.

Confucius answered: "An emperor should behave like emperor, a minister like minister, a father like father and a son like son."

Confucius' statement means that in the court the monarch is in supreme position and power, and his subjects or ministers should be subjected to him and do what he wants them to, and fulfill their duties respectively. The father in a family should run family affairs, love his children while the children should show filial respect to their parents and follow their orders. Confucius thought that under such rites and order, if abided by strictly, everyone could be in the proper place and love their careers; and every family would be in harmony, the society would be stable and the existing social system could stand firm forever. This is the concept of "zheng ming," meaning the rectification or reassuming of political and social order. Duke Jing had long been worrying about the disorderly status in society, so he naturally felt delighted in agreeing with Confucius' proposition.

"You are quite right, if the king isn't like a king, neither is the minister, the father and the son. Even though we have food, how could we eat it in peace!" Duke Jing said.

One spring, the State of Qi was afflicted with a severe drought. Many people suffered from hunger. Duke Jing asked Confucius, "What should I do in politics?"

"Economize on finance," Confucius answered simply. He suggested that the monarch should encourage frugality in every respect in time of disaster.

At the time, the State of Qi also was confronted by the threat of an attempted usurpation of power by senior officials, and the power of the monarch had become slack. The Tian Family had become a big threat to the monarch of Qi. These were the offspring of Chen Wan who years before had fled the State of Chen and changed the family name to Tian. The Tian family had taken control of the affairs of the state, expanding their power and buying people's support by dispensing favors. Duke Jing, who was now in dilemma, was quite satisfied with

Confucius' suggestion and — to show his belief and regard for Confucius — intended to grant a piece of land in Nixi to Confucius as his feud.

That Duke Jing bestowed favor on Confucius caused much trouble in this state. Some ministers were jealous of the privileges Confucius enjoyed and started to defame him. And Yan Ying was one of them.

Yan Ying, who styled himself Ping Zhong, was a native of Yiwei (present-day Gaomi County in Shandong Province). He assisted Duke Jing and had made great achievements in administering the internal affairs and safeguarding the dignity of the state. Yan Ying valued highly effectiveness and efficiency instead of empty talk on rites. On hearing that Duke Jing intended to give land in Nixi to Confucius, Yan Ying went to Duke Jing and said, "Now there is a group of people called the 'Ru' (later known as Confucianist) society. They love to pay lip service to high-sounding words but do not conduct business according to rules and regulations. They are too arrogant and complacent to be in an inferior position. They worry more about the dead than the living, proposing luxurious funeral arrangements even at the cost of one's family fortune, and we should do something to stop this trend. They roam from place to place to publicize their doctrine and make a living by sponging off aristocrats. Can we depend on these loafers to run our country? Since the decline of the Zhou Dynasty, have we ever seen any great sages? Only a few people understood the rites and the music. But now Confucius came and preached his doctrines, pretentiously giving people rules on what is proper and acceptable according to etiquette, like walking, kowtowing and bowing. How precise they are! I am afraid it would take one's whole life to study only a part of them, so it is impossible for you to change the status quo using his doctrines."

On the one hand, Yan Ying said what he did to persuade Duke Jing from granting Confucius land. On the other, what he said represented the opinion that many were holding towards Confucianism. Confucius and his followers stressed the importance of the rites system while the pragmatists such as Yan Ying stressed effectiveness. Duke Jing had wanted Confucius to advise on how to run the country to solve existing problems, but Yan Ying's remarks changed Duke Jing's mind. It now seemed true that Confucius' doctrines could not help him a lot; and more, so many people were opposing Confucius' idea. From that time on Duke Jing showed indifference towards Confucius.

Listening to Shao Music

Confucius sought asylum in the State of Qi not only for political reasons, but also for study and research. He had heard that in the State of Qi, there was preserved the "Shao" music of Shun's time. Soon after his arrival, he went to find it.

Confucius once had learned music from Chang Hong on his way to Luoyi where he learned rites or "Li" from Lao Zi. Confucius had asked Chang Hong, a famous musician of the time, about the music of "Da Wu" (the Great Martial for King Wu). Chang Hong was able to answer some of Confucius' questions, and Confucius also was able to add more to what he learned from Chang Hong. The music of "Da Wu" was a large-scale classic dance accompanied by music in the time of King Wu in the Zhou Dynasty. It is said that the dance was originally composed by Master Zhou when he drew up the rites and music. Through performance, the dance told stories about the course of King Wu's fight against King Zhou (the notorious tyrant): It related how to take a mass pledge, how to dispatch troops, how to fight and gain the victory in battle, how to return in triumph and how to run feudal states after victory. The dance was called "Ba Yi" (meaning "eight rows or files") with eight dancers in each row and each file, with 64 dancers all together.

The dancers perform with shields and jade hammers in hand, engrossing the audience in the solemn and lively performance. The dance fully revealed the early Zhou Dynasty spirit of gaining power with force, then running the country with benevolence and virtue. Since the Zhou Dynasty, the music of Da Wu had taken the place of "Shao" music. While many people praised and enjoyed the music of Da Wu, Confucius thought that an atmosphere of inherent aggressiveness kept it from being perfect. Since he was now in the State of Qi with the question "Is 'Shao' music better?" in mind, Confucius wanted to watch a performance of "Shao" music in person.

How is it that "Shao" music came to be preserved in the State of Qi? It was a long story: "Shao" was the music in the time of Shun, head of a significant ancient tribe in the east. He received the throne through Yao's abdication, having been chosen by Yao for his kindness and filial devotion. Confucius regarded both Shun and Yao as kings with virtue in ancient times. In his late years, with the interests of the nation in mind, Shun passed his throne to Yu, another sage, instead of to his own son Shang Jun. After the founding of Zhou Dynasty, King Wu of Zhou found Shun's descendants and granted the land of Chen (the present-day Huaiyang in Henan Province) to them as their fief. This was the State of Chen in the Zhou Dynasty.

In the early Spring and Autumn Period, when rebellion took place inside the State of Chen, Prince Wan of Chen had to flee to the State of Qi to seek support from Qi Huan Gong. He even changed his family name into Tian, so the later generations of Tian became the senior officials of Qi. Gradually, their power increased until they finally took over the power of the State of Qi. Owing to the prosperity of the Tians, the music of "Shao" made by Tian forefathers prevailed for a time. So when Confucius asked to see the music-dance of "Shao," his request was immediately granted. This made him very happy.

Confucius was so eager to attend the performance that he felt the carriage went too slowly. On his way, he kept urging the driver on by saying "Hurry up!" many times. When the music was being played, he was totally engrossed in it.

The original form of the "Shao" music, according to legend, was "Jiu Zhao" in Gao Xin Shi's time. Gao Xin Shi was the grandson of Huangdi, the Yellow Emperor. It was recorded that Gao Xin Shi had ordered Xian Hei to compose "Jiu Zhao," "Liu Lie" and "Liu Ying" which should be performed by such musical instruments as ox-hide drums and wooden drums, small drums, metal bells, chime stones, bamboo flutes and wind pipes, and

Xun, made from clay. The dancers costumed themselves as birds and beasts, with the leading dancer usually a phoenix or pheasant. In the dance, they fluttered and swooped, symbolizing peace and tranquility. One section in the dance is called one "Shao" and nine sections nine "Shaos." By the time of Shun, the 23-stringed plucked instrument and the "Xiao," a pipe-like instrument made of bamboo, were added to play the music, so the dance was also called "Xiao Shao Music Dance." In the *Book of Shang*, it says that "the music of Shao" is composed of nine sections, and the leading dancer was a phoenix while the rest were all other birds and beasts. When the birds were flying and the beasts were dancing, it was really a spectacular scene, while the musical instruments also imitated the sound of the birds and beasts. The whole dance was full of primitive romantic sentiment.

Following his enjoyment of the music-dance, Confucius was left intoxicated and enchanted. He was so much overwhelmed and carried away by the melody that he didn't enjoy meat as he used to for three months. The delight the mouth and stomach felt could not compete with the spiritual pleasure. This shows precisely Confucius' high taste for music. The music of "Shao" also reminded him of other musical works. In *The Analects, Eight Lines*, it says that "Confucius once said that Shao was perfect and beautiful, while Da Wu was beautiful but not perfect." The music in King Wu of Zhou was beautiful but it had a sound of aggressiveness bearing a strong sense of military domination, so it was not as good. While the music in Shun's time was beautiful as well but it embodied Shun's virtues in administering the nation with benevolence, which was the highest level in running a nation among the three ancient wise kings. Confucius' thought was manifested again in the course of his appreciation of music.

So when the later generations built "Shao Yuan," there was a place known as "Where Confucius listened to the Shao music" in the old city of Qi in honor of this incident. When people come to visit here, it seems that they can still hear the music of Shao and Confucius' doctrine of benevolence.

Yang Hu Staging a Revolt

Confucius accompanied Duke Zhao of Lu to the State of Qi to seek political asylum. Being dependent on others, Confucius couldn't help the King of Lu at all. And what's more, owing to the way Yan Ying and Confucius were at odds, Duke Jing of Qi changed his attitude towards Confucius. He was not as hospitable as before, and at last he said to Confucius, "I am aged and not so energetic as before. I'm sorry I am unable to send you to launch a reform in politics." Duke Jing of Qi's remarks shattered Confucius' dream of going into politics. Further, on hearing that someone wanted to do him harm, and urged by his disciples, Confucius left Qi in such a hurry that he couldn't cook the rice he had washed.

In 510 BC, Duke Zhao of Lu died in political asylum in Qianhou in the State of Jin. The second year after his death, his coffin was sent back to the State of Lu. Ji Sun Shi, who was then in power, buried him in the south of the graves of the officials in the State of Lu. This deprived Duke Zhao of the right to be buried in the same grave as his ancestors, which denoted that Duke Zhao of Lu was no longer treated as the king of Lu. What's more, Ji Sun Shi also intended to grant him a notorious title to make his offspring remember that he was not a good king. Ji Sun Shi's act of defying his superiors infuriated Confucius, so Confucius did all he could to call on others to respect Duke Zhao of Lu in many different ways. (For instance, some time later, he rebuilt the grave of Duke Zhao of Lu). Confucius also told the public that it was wrong for people to look down upon Duke Zhao, because it did not conform to the rites of the Zhou Dynasty.

In 505 BC, Ji Pingzi died and his son, Ji Huanzi succeeded to his throne. Like his father, Ji Huanzi controlled power second only to his father, but his power was not sufficient to relieve tensions inside the family. Some of his family subjects and Ji Huanzi's subordinates were not on good terms, of which, Zhong Liang Huai, Yang Hu and Gong Shan Bu Niu, were the most powerful. After Ji Pingzi's death, Yang Hu suggested that Ji Pingzi's "Pan Yu" (the jade he had worn when alive) should be buried together with him. But this was adamantly opposed by Zhong Liang Huai. In fact, Yang Hu and Zhong Liang Huai wanted to gain political advantage, and this eventually resulted in Yang Hu's driving Zhong Liang Huai away from the state of Lu, wiping out a powerful opponent. Yang Hu also killed He Miao, a member in the clan of the Ji Family, so as to threaten Ji Huanzi. Later, he kept Ji Huanzi in prison until he admitted defeat.

A few years before, Confucius could not stand the fact that Ji Pingzi had driven Duke Zhao of Lu out. And now he could hardly bear the similar fact that Yang Hu had kept Ji Huanzi in prison, nor could he agree to such behavior as defying one's elders or superiors.

Yang Hu thought Confucius would be on his side, for he had seen with his own eyes Confucius' reaction when Ji Sun Shi drove Duke Zhao of Lu away. He wanted to promote Confucius to be an official so as to win his support, but was rejected by him. Yang Hu did not realize that they held different views. Unlike Yang Hu, who intended to compete with his opponent for power, Confucius wanted to preserve the dignity of the king. One day, Yang Hu wanted to visit Confucius, so he sent someone to give him a small steamed pig as a present. Confucius accepted this gift with hesitation: On the one hand, it would be impolite to refuse to accept it, on the other hand Confucius was unwilling to be on Yang Hu's side. So Confucius went to call on him when Yang Hu was out. But unfortunately, Confucius happened to meet Yang Hu on his way back from the Yang's. Confucius was too nervous to say anything, but Yang Hu said many imposing words and urged Confucius not to hide his knowledge away, but to be an official. Otherwise, Confucius would miss many chances. Confucius had to agree with Yang Hu in words, but he never wanted to put that agreement into effect.

Three years later, with the rapid increase of Yang Hu's power, Yang Hu hoped to wipe out his opponents Meng Yizi, Su Shun Wu Shu, and Ji Huanzi, in collaboration with those dissatisfied with Ji Huanzi. He planned to take them over by getting rid of senior officials in the State of Lu. In October of that year, Yang Hu invited Ji Huanzi to have dinner with him at Puyuan so as to take this opportunity to kill him. At the news, Ji Huanzi escaped to Meng Sun Shi's home on his way to Puyuan. After this, Yang Hu staged a revolt and took hostage of Ding of Lu, Shu Sun Wu Shu and some others to fight against Meng Sun Shi, which, at last roused many nobles' opposition to Yang Hu. Finally, Yang Hu failed and fled to the State of Qi. Later he turned to Zhao Jianzi for help in the State of Jin, where he was appointed to an important position.

In this revolt, another family subject, Gong Shan Bu Niu, had responded to Yang Hu's call and rose up in Fei (the present-day Fei County in Shandong Province). Gong Shan Bu Niu admired Confucius' talent and had sent people to invite Confucius. Confucius was eager to put his talents into practice and find a place where he could govern the nation with his doctrine, so he wanted to have a try. His disciples, especially Zi Lu, couldn't understand Confucius. They thought it incredible for a person like Confucius to ally with a rebel subject. Confucius was always talking about his doctrine that "the prince is prince, and the minister is minister" and respect the king and the superior. Confucius explained to them, "Since he asked me to his place, can he want me to go there and do nothing? If he really wanted me, I could take this chance to realize my dream and construct another Eastern Zhou Dynasty."

Yang Hu was Ji Sun Shi's family subject, which belongs to "Shi," a social stratum in ancient China, between senior officials and the common people. In the late Spring and Autumn Period, the King of Zhou and dukes of the states were slave owners, and the senior officials were the prospective feudal landlord class. "Shi " belongs to the newly born landlord class, which depended on new means of exploitation to develop their power. Yang Hu was one of this class. Confucius didn't cooperate with the newly born landlord class, because he belonged to the class of slave owners. As for his intention to cooperate with Gong Shan was an embodiment of his overconfidence of himself and of his intention to change others with his doctrine.

Continuing Teaching

As a great educator, Confucius devoted his life to teaching, especially in his later years. As a matter of fact, his going into politics was part of his teaching, as was his traveling around the states seeking to be an official and doing research. But as a professional teacher, his teaching activities mainly had three phases: The first is when he started a private school in his thirties, but six or seven years later, he went to the State of Qi; the other is that in his later years, Confucius went back to teaching after he had traveled around the states, but that only lasted six or seven years. The longest time Confucius spent in teaching, with the greatest achievement, was in the decades from the time Confucius returned to the State of Lu to the period when he acted as the Prime Minister at Zhongdu. Many of his teaching methods and theories were formed in this period.

Like many educators in history, Confucius' teaching had two aspects — educating and teaching i.e., one is moral education and the other is intellectual education and technological education.

Moral education involves, first of all, cultivating

the character of the students. In ancient China, education was kept in the hands of slave owners and nobles. Common people, slaves and even medium and small slave owners were denied education. But by the end of the Spring and Autumn Period, many private schools had appeared and education had been extended to the common people. In his early years, in running education, Confucius put forward that "everyone has the right of receiving education." What he wanted to do was to educate the common people and organize a large intellectual group to depend on them as a power base to realize his political ambition. In a class society, all human activities were restricted to certain classes. The enlightenment education, which ultimately served the purpose of the ruling class, was closely related to politics. Confucius was conscious of this point, so he advocated in politics "to govern by virtue" and hoped to return to the flourishing age when "the old live in peace, friends are faithful and the young are enterprising," which was the real essence of education. He taught his students, "Study hard and be an official; and government officials should continue with all kinds of studies in their life time," which was his purpose of running a school. Confucius thought a ruler should keep on learning through all kinds of ruling experience, cultural knowledge and various techniques to fulfill the task of his class.

Learning was for going into politics and for

governing well. Learning was first. These ideas became Confucius' standard for his disciples, and they remained steady throughout his life in teaching. Confucius said, "At thirty I took my stand," which means at thirty, Confucius formed his views on politics. For a short time, his political ambition was realized but when he was forced to resign and leave the State of Lu to travel around the states, his main purpose was to seek an important position. When he came back, he worried about politics and trained his disciples to behave with morality and to learn virtues. All the means and criteria he created demonstrate his purpose of education.

Confucius had many suggestions and views on training people. In *The Analects*, Confucius said, "Setting the purpose in relation with the principle, the foundation of which is morality. Anything should be done in accordance with benevolence and the six arts should be learned, too." To Confucius, the aim of a man lies in realizing "Dao," the principle and morality. Dao was the basis for governing, while to fulfill the task of governing with virtues, one should know "benevolence," for "benevolence" embraced all of behavior and of how to create harmonious relations between people. But "benevolence" should be realized by learning the "six arts", i.e. rites, music, archery, charioteering, reading and writing and arithmetic. This is Confucius' idea about education, i.e. students should first set an aim, make clear the basis and set a criterion. This proposal outlines a track from ideal to action and represents Confucius' educational guidelines.

Confucius placed high value on moral education, but he thought intellectual education should be held in the same esteem. He trained and educated many excellent students and in his teaching, he summed up many valuable experiences in teaching materials and methods.

At Wuyu platform, south of Qufu, Confucius was always talking about ideals and ambition with his disciples. One day Confucius sat there with four disciples: Zi Lu, Zeng Xi, Ran You and Gong Xi Hua.

To them Confucius said:

"Don't be ill at ease because I am older than you. You often say your merits are not recognized. Now suppose someone was to recognize your merits, what employment would you choose?"

Zi Lu promptly and confidently replied, "Give me a country of a thousand war-chariots, hemmed in by powerful enemies, or even invaded by hostile armies, and suffered from famine. In the space of three years, I could restore its military power and bring prosperity to the country."

Confucius smiled at him and asked Ran You the same question. "Give me a domain sixty by seventy *li* or fifty by sixty *li*, and in the space of three years I shall make sure everybody has enough to eat."

"What about you, Gong Xi Hua?" Confucius turned to the youngest of the four.

Gong Xi Hua answered, "I am not sure if I could do this; but I am willing to learn. In ceremonies at the ancestral temple or at a conference or general gathering of the feudal princes I will wear my best ceremonial gown and play the part of junior assistant." Hearing that, Confucius didn't make any comments. He told Zeng Xi to talk about his ambitions.

Zeng Xi, who had been playing the zither, immediately stopped, rose and replied, "I fear my words will not be so well chosen as those of the other three."

Zeng Xi said, "In March when the sun is warm and bright, together with six or seven friends, I will bathe in the Yi River, enjoy the breeze on the Wuyu Platform and then go home singing."

Hearing this, Confucius was delighted, "This is what I want to do as well."

Confucius' proposal is right. He knew it was impossible to govern only by force, politics or diplomacy. Only by combining the three, can society remain stable and peaceful. Here Confucius' dream was shown clearly and so is the function of education.

Practicing His Ideas at Zhongdu

The revolt staged by Yang Hu in the state of Lu shocked Ji Huanzi, who was then in power. He came to realize the hard truth that the old etiquette and system should be kept and that to expand his force and strengthen his power, he should do something good in the state of Lu. Therefore, naturally Confucius became the ideal person he wanted. Confucius was famous in the state of Lu for his outstanding virtue and knowledge. Ji Huanzi concluded that since Confucius wouldn't cooperate with Yang Hu, he might just as well make friend with him. What's more, the brothers of Meng Sun Shi had become his students, which had gained the favor of Ji Huanzi and the Duke of Lu. So finally Ji Huanzi decided to put Confucius into an important position. In 501 BC, at the age of 51, Confucius was promoted to Prime Minister at Zhongdu. Undoubtedly, Confucius was delighted at having this chance to govern the country and go into politics, which had been the aim of his learning for so many years. Now the chance was at hand. He couldn't let this chance be lost, so he led some of his disciples to take office at Zhongdu.

A small town located in the northwest of the State of Lu, Zhongdu was rich in products and land. To its west was another small town called Kancheng. In 702 BC, Duke Huan of Lu traveled here and was attracted by the beautiful scenery. After watching meteorological phenomena and practicing divination, he told his entourage that after his death he would prefer to be buried here. The kings before Duke Huan of Lu such as Duke Wei, Hou, Xian, Zhen, Wu, Yi, Xiao, were all buried at the eastern side of Mount Fangshan, east of Lu City, but according to his wish, after Duke Huan's death, he was buried on the southern side of the Phoenix Hill, southwest of Kancheng. Then the kings after him such as Zhuang, Min, Xi, Wen, Xuan, Chen, and Xiang were all buried here, too. An exception was Duke Zhao of Lu for he died at Qianhou, but before long, he was also buried here.

Kancheng was directly under the jurisdiction of Zhongdu, which was both an important town in the State of Lu and the burial land of the eight kings of Lu. That Confucius was sent here to work as an official shows he was highly respected and honored.

After he arrived at Zhongdu, Confucius implemented many new measures with his disciple Ran Boniu. The first measure he took related to respecting the elderly. Confucius regarded "assuring that the old live in peace" as his criterion of an ideal world. In order to let the elderly spend their final years in happiness, Confucius thought the first thing was to respect them — for respecting the old was respecting history, knowledge and experience. Based on the principle of "the old and the young should have different food," Confucius decided that people of 50 should have fine grain; the people of 60 or 70 should have meat and people of 80 or 90 should be taken care of. As for babies, they also should be given fine food so as to make them grow rapidly. The second measure was: "The weak and the strong should have different positions respectively." The purpose of this measure was to encourage all people to participate according to their abilities. At that time, agricultural production was the most important task, and young men mainly engaged in agricultural field work. Those excellent in their work should be praised, and the lazy punished. Some people were also permitted work in the handicraft industry. Whatever the work, improvement depended on constant reevaluation of technology and design of better tools. Outside of production, cultural activity was important, too. Confucius always told his disciples that their main task was to learn the rules, cultivate their moral character and nourish their nature so as to be able to administer the country and make the whole country peaceful. The different positions, as a matter of fact, amounted to division of labor in society, no doubt a progressive idea at the time.

In order to develop production, Confucius put emphasis on the principle of not making bogus products as he took to rectify the economic order. He said that given that the world is so big there could be no definite regulation about what is good and what is bad. However, there is a universal rule that all people should follow: Faith. People love to keep on good terms with a man who shows faith. A governor should be faithful to his people, and a businessman should be faithful to his customers. When making goods, a manufacturer should guarantee quality and not use any cheap thing to take the place of the good. In the State of Lu, a sheep trader — called Shen You Shi — fed his sheep grass soaked in salty water. The thirsty sheep drank water desperately, and thus gained weight to help Shen You Shi earn quite a lot of money. Confucius educated this man on the immorality of his cheating people, and Confucius also severely punished him. Through these two approaches, Confucius rehabilitated a tradesman who had been engaging in deceptive practices.

In ancient times, funeral ceremonies were given much attention. Among the 300 rites of Zhou and 3,000 etiquettes — most had to do with funeral ceremonies. Take a coffin, for instance. In accordance with the rites of Zhou, kings were supposed to have one coffin and four "guo," a larger coffin outside the small one, while the various marquis were to have one coffin and three guos; senior officials one coffin and two guos. These coffins were very thick and strong. To cut down on expenses and change funeral customs, Confucius ordered that a coffin should be 2.4 inches thick and a guo 3 inches. Anyone violating the regulation would be subject to punishment. Lavish funerals were also put under control. In Confucius' mind, the graves in the Xia, Shang and Zhou dynasties usually extended above the surface of ground, wasting arable land. He suggested that graves should not project above the surface of the ground nor should trees be planted around the site. In the past, once land was used for a grave, ploughing on top of it was forbidden. But now under Confucius' regulations, it became legal to grow crops on such land. These proposals to us may seem easy to carry out, but in ancient times, they could hardly have been implemented without firm resolution.

A couple of years ago Duke Zhao of Lu was driven out of the State of Lu and died in exile. His coffin was sent back for burial in the State of Lu. But there, the man now in power — Ji Sun Shi — took revenge on Duke Zhao even after death by burying him to the south of the graves of dukes of Lu, denying him the right to enter his ancestral burial ground. This revealed that Ji Sun Shi did not recognize Duke Zhao as a king of Lu. One of Ji

Sun Shi's senior officials called Jia He tried his best to persuade Ji Sun Shi not to do that, but Ji Sun Shi did not accept Jia He's advice. Then Confucius was appointed as the Prime Minister at Zhongdu, and he was eager to reclaim the reputation of Duke Zhao of Lu. He had a long ditch dug on the south, east and west of the tomb of Duke Zhao. In this way, though the grave of Duke Zhao of Lu was far from that of the dukes of Lu, nevertheless it was linked to the graves of the dukes of Lu, thus indicating it as a king's grave. The ditch was called by later generations "Confucius' ditch."

Besides the attention he gave to politics and the economy during his tenure as Prime Minister at Zhongdu, Confucius also paid much attention to local education for the common people. Owing to Confucius' great achievements in education and his tolerant and generous policies, people lived a happy life. Many did not bother to bolt their doors at night and no one picked up things left by the wayside. After only a year in office, Confucius' outstanding abilities in running the town affairs attracted many people to come to learn from him.

Duke Ding of Lu was very pleased at Confucius' success in being an official. He asked, "Can your methods be learned and used in other places?" Confucius answered proudly, "They can be applied everywhere and are not limited to the State of Lu."

In Zhongdu — present-day Wenshang in Shandong Province — there exist many relics left by Confucius when he was an official there as well as some monuments built by people who hoped to memorialize Confucius and remember the feats of the sage.

Promoted to Be Head of the Department of Justice in the State of Lu

Because of his excellent work in politics as Prime Minister in Zhongdu, Confucius was promoted to be the Minister of Works by Duke Ding of Lu.

Minister of Works or Minister of Engineering was a stipulated official post in the rites of Zhou. In *Confucius' Family Quotations*, it is recorded that Confucius could recognize the Five Lands (The "Five Lands" referred to mountains and forests, swamps, hills, plateau and plains.) and by treating according to their respective characteristics enable each to prosper. Confucius was skillful in management and knew how to cultivate the land and grow crops according to the conditions of the land. As he was devoted to his duty as Minister of Works Confucius soon got another promotion.

In 500 BC, the 10th year of Duke Ding of Lu, Confucius was appointed as Great Minister of Justice in the State of Lu. According to the chapter

"Minister of Justice" in *Rites of Zhou,* Minister of Justice was an important official: It was on the same level with Minister of Education and Minister of War and because of its dignity in administering law and justice, it was called Great Minister of Justice as well. The responsibilities of Great Minister of Justice included managing the three statutes of the state and helping the king to run the country. Confucius served as Prime Minister in Zhongdu only one year, Minister of Works three months but Minister of Justice three years. It was his best time in politics.

Since the Minister of Justice was in charge of tracking down and arresting thieves and judging criminals, trying cases was a main task. At that time, there were no formal judiciary procedures and people in general were kept in the dark about the law. Therefore, custom was often referred to in making a judgment when trying a case. Of course, the custom often found itself on the side of aristocrats. In ancient China, there was a saying that "senior officials are exempt from punishment." Whenever there was a lawsuit between aristocrats and common people, the aristocrats often had the advantage. After taking office as the Minister of Justice, Confucius began to change the way cases were tried. He would never try a case without investigating its causes and outcome, relations, subjective and objective terms and something about prosecutor and defender. In order to understand the actual situation, Confucius was always going to the common people to search for witnesses and evidences so as to draw a correct conclusion and conduct a fair hearing. Confucius advocated the virtues of humanity and morality and opposed struggling and fighting. Once a father and son came to court at the same time. They were both in an agitated mood. The son said angrily that he treated his father very well, but his father was often losing his temper, cursing him in public and at times even beating him so that he felt inferior to others. But the father said that his son was not filial. When his wife died, he painstakingly brought his son up until he got married but after that, his son changed a lot. Though he provided him with food and clothes, he didn't respect him much and often ordered him to do this and to do that. As a result, he didn't feel good and no wonder he often flew into a rage.

In ancient China, it was odd for a son to sue his father. Ji Huanzi suggested killing the son, but Confucius kept the son in prison for three months. He said to the son, "You raise many dogs and horses. You think it is natural to order them around, but if you don't respect your father and often tell him to do this and to do that, what's the difference between him and those dogs and horses? Everyone should show filial piety to his parents. Providing him with enough food doesn't mean that you respect your father and are filial to him. Your father lost his temper and embarrassed you in public because he didn't feel happy. After all, it is you who are to blame." He then said to the father, "After all, he is your son. What good will it do if you make your son embarrassed and humiliate him in public? If I had him killed, who would support you when you become old?"

Confucius' remarks moved the father and son deeply so that the father withdrew his accusation and the son confessed that it was his fault for treating his father badly. When the father and the son met each other, they cried and hugged each other tight. With that, Confucius set the son free. He took the chance to educate the common people; therefore he enjoyed a high reputation there.

As an official in charge of justice, Confucius never misused punishment. He preferred compassion to punishment. Confucius said, "To govern by virtue is like the pole-star which holds its place, and around which the multitude of stars revolve." He also said, "Don't always control the common people with administrative decrees and punish them with penalties. If you do so, it will only make people develop the idea of leaving things to chance and disregarding shame. If you guide them by virtue in politics and restrain them by rites, they will have the idea of shame and follow you in the way you lead."

Since Confucius handled legal cases impartially, the number of lawsuits in the State of Lu kept declining and Confucius was delighted. But when he tried a case and saw the miserable conditions of the victims and those who were punished by law, Confucius felt very sad. He said meaningfully: "Dealing with lawsuits, I consider it my duty to judge them impartially and see that justice is done. But this is not a job I would find difficult to part with. How I wish people's morality would be improved and there would be no cheating and quarreling and no more lawsuits ever! If so, the world would be stable and peaceful."

Confucius was strict with himself. Though he was an official in government, he acted kindly toward people rather than scolding and lecturing them. But when he discussed politics and plans for running the country at court, he was eloquent, bold and discreet. He treated those in high positions according to the rites and never feared those with power. And to those inferior in social status, Confucius was always kind and amiable.

Confucius stressed appointing men with superior abilities and never abused power for personal gain. He recommended and promoted some able men, but his son Kong Li was not an official. It was not because Kong Li was not competent but because Confucius was an honest and incorruptible official..

As the Great Minister of Justice, Confucius was not only in charge of criminal procedures but also provided consulting services for the people of the upper class in the State of Lu. Once, Duke Ding of Lu asked him, "What's the principle concerning a ruler's use of his ministers and a minister's serving his ruler?" Confucius answered by saying, "A ruler in employing his ministers should be guided solely by the prescriptions of ritual. Ministers in serving their ruler, solely by devotion to his cause. If a ruler acts according to the rites, then ministers are supposed to be faithful to him. If a ruler does not act according to the rites, it is OK for his ministers to disobey him." Confucius cited King Zhou of Shang as an example. In his answer Confucius was attempting to advise Duke Ding of Lu to be a self-disciplined ruler. Duke Ding was not happy with Confucius' remarks, but he couldn't say a word.

Once the king of Lu asked Confucius, "It is said that what a king said is suffice to save or destroy a country. Is that right? " Confucius answered, "It is right and wrong. To say a country is saved or destroyed by one remark of the ruler is an exaggeration — so it's wrong. But it is true that if a ruler governs the country diligently, appoints able men, adopts good suggestions — the country will be prosperous. This is to say that one remark could save a country. And if a ruler is keen on his power regardless of suggestions and persuasions, probably the country would perish at his hand. This is to say that one remark could ruin a country. Of course, one remark here does not refer to one sentence but rather to the remarks and conduct of a ruler. Therefore, a ruler is supposed to be careful about his remarks and conduct." Confucius' above remarks also intended to persuade king of Lu to do good things, but they were not accepted by him.

Meeting of Sovereigns at Jiagu

As the Great Minister of Justice of Lu, Confucius had attended the meeting of sovereigns at Jiagu, which was a bilateral meeting between the states of Qi and Lu and a successful diplomatic function as well.

The merits Confucius had achieved in the State of Lu threatened its neighboring country, Qi. Li Chu, a minister of Qi, suggested to Duke Jing of Qi, "King of Lu put Confucius in an important position and now he has made great achievements and before long, he is sure to be successful in politics. Then sooner or later, the State of Lu will become a threat to us. But Confucius has no courage except for knowing the rites, therefore, we should invite the king of Lu to a meeting and force the State of Lu to surrender to us. We will have our army wait in ambush to kidnap the king and force him to surrender." Duke Jing adopted Li Chu's suggestion and sent an emissary to Lu to set the date and the place for a meeting. Confucius was appointed master of ceremony responsible for the meeting at Jiagu (present-day Laiwu). Beforehand,

Confucius had warned Duke Ding, "I heard that a country should have military backing in diplomacy and vice versa. In ancient times, whenever the kings went on an diplomatic mission, they were always followed by their guards. I hope you send your Minister of War to go with you with some soldiers and war chariots." Finally, Duke Ding of Lu accepted his suggestion.

In the 10th year of Duke Ding of Lu's reign (500 BC), at Jiagu, east of Mount Tai, the rulers of Qi and Lu had a meeting with their respective ministers. They bowed and proposed toasts to each other on the three-flight earthen platform. As soon as they sat down, one servant of the State of Qi announced the playing of the music, "four directions." To this, Duke Jing agreed before Duke Ding could say anything. After that a number of natives of the eastern tribes, holding up various banners, shields, spears, swords, and halberds, came forward. On that urgent occasion, Confucius had to come out to stop them. In fact, on such a formal occasion, Confucius was supposed, according to his status, to walk only one step at a time, and then only after one foot had come side-by-side with the other, could he walk down another flight. But the situation was so urgent that Confucius flew down three flights regardless of his place, waving the long sleeve of his robe, and shouting, "Why is foreign music and dance of the eastern tribes being played on this occasion of the kings of two states holding a meeting?" He interrogated the man in charge, demanding him to do something about it before Duke Jing dismissed the musicians and dancers. After a while, the man in charge announced that court music would be played, and Duke Jing immediately gave permission to do it before Duke Ding of Lu responded. Then a group of men in various clothes and costumes, tall and short, handsome and ugly, jumped and ran to the platform. Confucius strode over two flights and said in a stern voice, "Anyone who disrespects officials should be killed according to the law, please do it now!" What Confucius referred to was some of the regulations in the rites of Zhou. The judge couldn't say anything but followed Confucius' order and killed the leader of the dancers.

Their attempt to kidnap the king of Lu failed, Li Chu and his men asked for the addition of one item to the book of alliance, i. e. if the State of Qi goes out to battle, the State of Lu will send 300 war chariots to accompany them and follow their orders or be punished. Confucius also put forward an item agreeing to the State of Qi's terms but only after "you have returned the land of Wenyang seized from Lu to us." Confucius' response caught Duke Jing of Qi off guard.

In the meeting at Jiagu, Confucius argued strongly based on the rites of Zhou. His prompt decision

defeated the scheme of Qi's intending to kidnap and kill the king of Lu. After the meeting, Duke Jing of Qi asked to give a banquet in honor of Duke Ding of Lu, but this was declined by Confucius to avoid any incidents.

Duke Jing of Qi came back and complained to his ministers, "Confucius assisted the king of Lu with the rules of noble man, but you taught me with rules of barbarians that made me offend the State of Lu and lose face. What, do you think, I should do?" Some ministers said, "The noble man should correct his wrongs. Only small men are always looking for excuses. If you regret what you have done, you should follow the rules of a noble man and take action to express your regret." So Duke Jing of Qi returned the land seized by Qi from Lu to the State of Lu to make up for his error.

Confucius' victory in the meeting at Jiagu rests greatly on his hard work in learning rites and literature, his profound knowledge and his ability of putting knowledge into practical use. By stepping forward bravely in times of emergency, he demonstrated his firm, persistent and quick-witted character and outstanding political ability. This meeting raised Confucius' dignity greatly within his state.

Causing Trouble by Suggesting Demolishing the Manors of Senior Officials

The meeting of the sovereigns at Jiagu, a rare victory in diplomacy, created a relatively stable situation for the state of Lu. Confucius, who had gained great honor for his country at the meeting, naturally enjoyed respect and admiration from people. Once he was in power, Confucius was inclined to preach his year-long proposal of respecting and being loyal to the sovereign so as to raise the social status of the king of Lu. One means was to suppress the senior officials who were struggling for power against the king of Lu.

In Lu, the power of both the senior officials and their family subjects had been increasing, especially the power of the family subjects which was inclining to surpass that of their masters. In their own feuds, they built high walls. This not only violated etiquette and exceeded authority but posed a direct threat to the king of Lu. Confucius intended to uproot the latent danger.

In the summer of the 12th year in the reign of Duke Ding of Lu (498 BC), Confucius said to Duke Ding, "According to regulations in the rites of Zhou, an official shouldn't have an army nor should a senior official have a city with an area of 5 *li*." The city walls Confucius wanted to demolish were the City of Cheng (in present-day Ningyang County in Shandong Province), the City of Hou (in present-day Dongping County in Shandong Province) and the City of Fei (in present-day Fei County in Shandong Province). The masters in the three cities each owned lands, armies and shared power with the king of Lu. Confucius' proposal of enhancing the king's power benefited the State of Lu and was naturally supported by Duke Ding of Lu. To everyone's surprise, Ji Sun Shi, owner of the City of Fei, supported Confucius' proposal. At that time, Gong Shan Bu Niu, Ji Sun Shi's family subject occupied the Fei City. To eliminate Gong Shan Bu Niu and extricate himself from the trouble, Ji Sun Shi adopted Confucius' proposal. With the king of Lu and Ji Sun Shi's support, Confucius had confidence and began to demolish the walls of the three cities. His student Zi Lu was sent to Ji Sun Shi's family as a steward, supposed to do something from within. The Hou City owned by Shu Sun Shi, the weakest among the three cities, was first to be demolished. The Fei City of Ji was pulled down under Ji Huanzi's support. But Gong Shan Bu Niu and

Shu Sun Zhe rose up and fought against them at the City of Fei up to the foot of the City of Lu. Duke Ding of Lu was so frightened that he hid at the platform of Ji Wu Zi in the palace of Ji Shi. Though Gong Shan Bu Niu's army couldn't break into the city, their arrows had even reached near Duke Ding of Lu. On hearing the news, Confucius immediately had Shen Ju Xu and Le Qi lead an army to fight against Gong Shan Bu Niu and defeated him. Gong Shan Bu Niu was chased to Gumie (present-day Sishui in Shandong Province). The Fei City was pulled down and the State of Lu won at last.

After the cities of Hou and Fei were demolished by force, only Cheng City remained occupied by Meng Sun Shi. But Gong Lian Chu Fu, army commander of Cheng City, had been loyal to Meng Sun Shi, so Meng Sun Shi couldn't find reasons to attack him. When Confucius ordered them to pull down their walls, Gong Lian Chu Fu said to Meng Sun Shi: "The Cheng City shouldn't be demolished, for your feud is close to the State of Qi. If it is pulled down, they will attack it from the north. To demolish Cheng City will ruin Meng Sun Shi." He warned Meng Sun Shi not to be taken in by the sweet words of others, saying if Meng Sun Shi followed the other two, he would leave himself in a very difficult situation. Meng followed Gong's proposal and refused to demolish the city.

The reason why the City of Cheng is hard to attack is because what Gong Lian Chu Fu had said — "to demolish the city will ruin Meng Sun Shi," — had touched Meng greatly. It also affected the families of Shu Sun Shi and Ji Sun Shi. At last, they realized that Confucius' real intention was to uproot their base and power, although he helped them get rid of their rebellious subjects. They refused to support Confucius when they found they had been cheated, thus Confucius' plan of demolishing the three cities failed.

Confucius was overcome with disappointment at the failure of strengthening the central power by taking power away from the ministers, but his proposal was refused by many senior officials. As a result, many nobles in Lu lost their confidence in him and besides, he had made many enemies in the state, which surely became a latent danger for him.

Previously, Ji Huanzi had been very kind to Confucius. However, Confucius' actions such as demolishing the three cities and digging the ditch around the grave of Duke Zhao of Lu and resuming his reputation and showing great respect to the king of Lu — all this made Ji Huanzi realize that Confucius was not on his side. After that, Ji Huanzi was cold to Confucius.

Among Confucius' disciples, Meng Yi Zi, the offspring of Meng Sun Shi, Nangong Jing Shu and Gong Boliao went against Confucius and said many bad things about him to Ji Huanzi. Finally it made Zi Lu lose his post and Confucius' authority in the State of Lu was diminished greatly.

Confucius was disappointed and angry and became seriously ill. When Duke Ding of Lu called on him, he was so sick that he couldn't sit up but could only cover himself with a robe worn whenever he came to court to show his respect for the king. Shortly after that, Zi Fu Jing Bo, a senior official came to see Confucius and told him that Gong Boliao had informed against Zi Lu and had made many irresponsible remarks. Zi Fu Jing Bo suggested having Gong Boliao killed, only to be refused by Confucius. He said, "The success or failure of our proposition depends on fate. What can the inferior Gong Boliao do to us?" After this failure, Confucius still had confidence in his own career.

Leaving Lu

Confucius' failed attempt to demolish the three
city walls had created many opponents inside the
State of Lu, and the people in power in the State of
Qi were his enemies as well. Soon after the sovereign meeting at Jiagu, Duke Jing of Qi passed away
and Yan Ying was still in power. Li Chu, who would
not resign himself to defeat at the sovereign meeting at Jiagu, put forward a proposal to the king of
Qi that would drive a wedge between Confucius
and the king of Lu.

In Confucius' whole life, he had been observing
the rites of Zhou, as had been shown in managing
the State of Lu. He demanded that the king and his
officials be discreet in words and deeds, and develop
a good moral integrity. He warned them of keeping
away from sycophants, and he was strongly against
their wallowing in luxury and pleasure. In Confucius' mind, not only did such behavior not conform
to the rites of Zhou but it also would be likely to
cause great trouble — especially in a situation where
political corruption was more serious with greedy
aristocrats struggling for their own enjoyment. To

take advantage of Duke Ding of Lu and Ji Huanzi's liking for amusements, the State of Qi selected 80 beautiful girls in beautiful clothes who were skillful in decadent music. These girls and 120 horses covered with shining silks were sent to the king of Lu.

Many people in Lu were attracted by the 80 beautiful girls and 120 good horses stationed beyond the south gate and even Ji Huanzi himself couldn't resist the temptation and three times went to see them. No doubt, Duke Ding of Lu wanted to accept these gifts right away but he felt it difficult to decide, for Confucius had told him for many times that this didn't conform to the rites of Zhou.

When Confucius heard about this, at first, he had wanted to persuade the king of Lu to act in righteousness but lost confidence when he saw the king was so greedy and Ji Huanzi's persuasion so intensive. Many of his disciples thought this was against Confucius' belief and disrespectful to their master. Therefore, they said to Confucius, "Master, we can't assist the king, let's leave here, shall we?" Confucius was excited, and he said, "Women and people of low birth are very hard to deal with. If you are friendly with them, they get out of hand, and if you keep your distance, they resent it." Confucius meant that the girls sent by the State of Qi and those wicked small men including the immoral Ji Huanzi were difficult to deal with.

Confucius did not accept the proposal that he

leave Lu. He said to his disciples, "We may as well wait and see. They are going to offer sacrifices and if they send me as usual the sacrificial meat, this will show that they still respect me. We'd better wait and see." Heaven sacrifice was the highest of rites. After the sacrifice, the sacrificial meat made by pig, sheep and cattle was sent to the officials by the king. This act was called "offering sacrificial meat." According to Confucius' rank in court, he was entitled to get the sacrificial meat, but unfortunately Confucius didn't receive it because of his failure in demolishing the three city walls and becoming an enemy of aristocrats in Lu, as well as his opposition to accepting the beautiful girls. He waited for three days but no one came to offer sacrificial meat.

Confucius thought what he had done in Lu according to the rites of Zhou was nothing but to start a career and that these people in power were hopeless and that he should stop at once while the condition was still good. If he still insisted on his proposals, he would be destined to be in a passive condition and couldn't back down with good grace. So he thought he had better leave and try to find another enlightened ruler to carry out his political aspirations. Confucius was in low spirits when the time came for him to leave Lu, his native land. He felt sad that he was unable to carry out his political decrees. When he rode slowly with his disciples in a carriage and arrived at Tun, south of Lu, Shi Yi, a musician of Lu caught up with him and said to Confucius, "Master, it's not your fault you have to leave here." Confucius said thoughtfully, "What can I say, I'd better sing a song for you." Then he sang, "These seductive women could drive such a talent of managing the country like me to a strange land. And their decadent music could destroy our country. I have to spend the unlucky days leisurely."

It is recorded in some books that before Confucius left Lu, he composed a song called "A Song for Gui Mountain." The lyrics go: "I wanted to look back at Lu, but it was blocked by Gui Mountain. And because I had no power in hand, what could I do about it? "

The reference to Gui Mountain was to the ruling Ji family. It was their rule that stopped Confucius from carrying out his ideas about how to govern a country.

Qi's strategem of sowing discord and the adversaries in Lu made it impossible for Confucius to stay there any longer to try to realize his political aspirations. So Confucius had to leave Lu for other states to preach his political theories. In the thirteenth year of the reign of Duke Ding of Lu (497 BC), Confucius began to travel across the various states at the age of 54, and the travel lasted 14 years.

A Narrow Escape at the City of Kuang and City of Pu

After leaving the State of Lu, Confucius went to other states in the hope of realizing his political ambition. But, where should he go? The manor of Ji was in the east and the State of Qi, which had been trying to alienate him from his motherland, was in the north. The State of Zhu and the State of Xiaozhu in the south were in turmoil. As a result, he arrived in the State of Wei in the west as his first stop. The State of Wei in the Spring and Autumn Period was located in Puyang, Henan Province. It was the manor of Kangshu, younger brother of King Wu of the Zhou Dynasty. Therefore, Wei and Lu were closely related "brother states." The king ruling Wei at that time was Ling Gong who had been the king for 38 years. Also, Zi Lu's brother-in-law, Yan Zhuozou was one of the favorite ministers of Duke Ling of Wei. So, Confucius and his students decided to stop first in the State of Wei, a peaceful state.

For many years, Confucius' action of leading his students to leave his motherland for other states was known as "touring across the states." As a matter of fact, it should be properly called "visiting other states trying to get a position in a government department." Their traveling was actually a kind of political activity. This group of people led by Confucius was not a tourist group, nor was it an educational organization. The 14 years they spent in other states was actually full of their political activities.

After he reached the State of Wei, Confucius sat in a carriage driven by one of his students, Ran You. While he was travelling, he observed the scenes along the journey. One day, when they saw the state was densely populated, Confucius suddenly blurted out, "What a large number of people!"

Ran You asked: "After they have increased to such a large number, what should the government do with them?"

"Make them rich," Confucius answered.

"When they get rich, what should the government do next?" Ran You asked.

"Educate them!"

Confucius' two responses to Ran You's questions showed his belief in governing a state, that is, by following a process of making people numerous, rich and educated. This reveals to us that Confucius paid much more attention to the improvement of economic conditions although he also stressed the importance of building up of the superstructure, i.e., the education of people, which he believed should be based on a comfortable life for the common people.

When Confucius and his students arrived at the State of Wei, one of his students, Zi Lu visited his brother-in-law, Yan Zhuozou, through whom, they got the opportunity to meet Duke Ling of Wei, who reigned from 534 BC to 493 BC. At first, Duke Ling of Wei did not know Confucius very well. He welcomed him and his students respectfully only because they were a unique group of majestic looking people who came from afar. As the "scholars" of the society at that time, they could depend on their own abilities to lobby around in many states, which made them very similar to advisors in later times. People received those scholars because they wanted to find more counselors who would discuss with them ways of governing the state. By welcoming those scholars, they could also win a better reputation by demonstrating to people that they were wise, upright and honest rulers who were very eager to recruit talented people by paying them proper respect. In view of this, Duke Ling of Wei asked Confucius and his students to stay in his state and paid him the same salary as he had received in the State of Lu.

As an underdeveloped state, the State of Wei looked relatively peaceful because rising forces had not gained enough power. But the actual situation was just the opposite. In the second year after Confucius arrived in the state, an armed rebellion led by Gongsun Xu, an aristocrat and high official of Wei, broke out. Although this rebellion was soon put down by forces sent by Duke Ling of Wei — and although Gongsun Xu was driven back to the City of Pu and City of Kuang, two of his manors — the rule of Duke Ling of Wei was shaken. When the rebellion was going on, Confucius was suspected and envied by some officials because he received a good salary without giving his contribution to the state.

"Confucius came to our state with so many students," someone said to Duke Ling of Wei one day, "but no one knows what they are trying to do here. What shall we do if they do something dangerous to our state?"

Duke Ling of Wei, a man with no definite view of his own who easily believed whatever he heard, found these words reasonable. So he sent a man named Gongsun Jia to keep watch on Confucius and his students. After they heard about it, Confucius and his students considered this as an insult. They decided that it would no longer be convenient for them to live in a state where people could so easily find an excuse to accuse them of wrongdoings. Thus, they stayed in the State of Wei for only 10 months before leaving.

In 497 BC, Confucius and his students left Wei

for the State of Chen which was located in the south. On their way to Chen, they met some trouble in Kuang City (west of present-day Sui County in Henan Province). Gongsun Xu, the aristocrat of the State of Wei, had been exiled to this place after his failed rebellion, and he was in constant fear of being caught by people sent by Duke Ling of Wei. When Gongsun Xu saw such a large number of people coming from Wei, he suspected that Confucius and his students had been dispatched by Duke Ling of Wei to arrest him. To make things worse, Confucius looked a lot like Yang Hu from the State of Lu, a very tall man like Confucius who had caused trouble locally. Besides, as they were passing along, Yan Ke, a student who was driving the carriage with a whip in his hand, talking to Confucius, "Yang Hu and I fought our way into Kuang from this pass." The local people heard his words and took them as the gang of Yang Hu, who had caused them so much trouble. So people passed the word from one to another, and — to defend themselves — they surrounded Confucius and his students.

Confucius, together with his students, did not know why they had been surrounded by so many people. Confucius sent some of his students to find out the reason and to negotiate with the local people. At the same time, he encouraged his students by saying, "After the death of Emperor Zhou Wen Wang, the cultural heritage of human beings has been entrusted to us, right? If God wanted to destroy this heritage, he would not have placed it into our hands; if God didn't want to eradicate this heritage, what can Kuang people do to us?" These words show us that Confucius was quite conceited. In addition, Confucius said what he did to encourage his students to overcome the difficulties.

After being surrounded for five days, Confucius and his students felt baffled. While he was counting the number of his students, he suddenly found that his beloved student, Yan Hui had disappeared, which made him very worried. Soon, Yan Hui returned.

"You are back at last," said Confucius, "I thought you must have been dead."

"Since you are still here," said Yan Hui, "how dare I die so easily?"

What Yan Hui said demonstrates to us his determination to assist Confucius in carrying out his great ambition in the future.

Reasoning with people had been Confucius' way to deal with conflict. So, he decided to try to solve the problem through peaceful means before resorting to force. However, no matter how hard he tried to explain the situation to the Kuang people, they refused to listen to him or to leave. On the contrary, they took turns surrounding Confucius and his students.

Gong Liang Ru was one of Confucius' students who had followed him with five carriages and his

family. Besides learning from Confucius like other students, he also practiced martial arts in his spare time. Now it was time for him to use what he had learned. So with five chariots, he fought with the Kuang people. When Gongsun Xu realized that they were not people sent by Duke Ling of Wei, he stopped fighting with them. People who had been surrounding Confucius and his students were common people in the City of Kuang. As they were unorganized and they were not capable of fighting for a long time, they were defeated as soon as Gongsun Xu turned on them. Only in this way did it become possible for Confucius and his students to leave Kuang. However, when they reached the City of Pu (Changyuan County in Henan Province), they were again surrounded by the local people.

The City of Pu was the military base of Gongsun Xu, and he did not want the king of Wei to know the actual situation there. Since Confucius and his students had arrived and had found out their actual condition, Gongsun Xu wouldn't let them go so easily. So, the two parties decided to negotiate. Pu people said that Confucius and his students could leave the City of Pu on the condition that they would not report the actual condition in the city to the king of Wei after they left. Although Confucius agreed to this, he returned to the State of Wei as soon as he left Pu. Instead of keeping the secret as he had promised, he told the king of Wei everything he saw in Pu. This confused his student Zi Lu who asked, "Didn't we just sign the agreement with Pu people? Why didn't we carry out our agreement?"

"We were forced to sign this agreement," said Confucius, "Of course, we should not keep it. Even if God knows what we have done, he will not blame us."

Four Years in the State of Wei

Confucius and his students had planned to leave the State of Wei for the south, but after encountering so many difficulties in their journey, they decided to stay in the State of Wei for a while. By doing so, Confucius could try to persuade the king to change his misunderstanding of him. Furthermore, Confucius hoped that he could one day make good use of his skills to govern the state.

An elderly minister in the State of Wei named Qu Boyu often told Confucius that he wanted to be his student, but Confucius treated him just as an old friend. Confucius had praised him, saying, "A true gentleman takes office in the government when the king rules his state with wisdom and justice, but when the king is no longer wise or just, he should retire and live in seclusion. Qu Boyu is a gentleman of this kind." Confucius had also complimented him because Qu Boyu understood himself well and knew the importance of "making up for his mistakes." So, when Confucius and his students returned to the State of Wei, they asked Qu Boyu to arrange their accommodations.

Confucius and his students stayed in the State of Wei for three years this time. During these three years, Duke Ding of Lu died and was succeeded by his son Ji Jiang, who was also known as Duke Ai of Lu. Because Duke Ai of Lu was just enthroned, he was not ready to carry out any new policies, which made Confucius' returning to his motherland not worthwhile. But, what was the situation like in the State of Wei, where he stayed? Duke Ling of Wei was an indecisive and silly king who kept his nation intact only by getting assistance from his ministers. He accepted Confucius and showed proper respect for him and his students only because he wanted to show to others that he treated the wise people courteously. Although he achieved nothing in politics, he enjoyed indulging in drink and living an extravagant life. In his later years, he got a new concubine named Nan Zi with whom he spent most of his time each day squandering his life.

As Duke Ling of Wei's favorite concubine, Nan Zi was a young and fairly attractive woman who found it boring to live with such an old man. On the other hand, Duke Ling of Wei's position was the highest in the state, so she was lucky to have found favor in his eyes — something difficult for a commoner to do. As time passed and Nan Zi grew tired of living in the lonely palace, she made it her ambition to get into politics. Several years previously, she had heard that in the State of Lu there was a wise and kind scholar named Kong Qiu (Confucius). Since then, she had been trying to get to know him so as to raise her status. Confucius, on the other hand, also wanted to know her because Duke Ling of Wei showed no trust in him though Confucius had endured hardships to travel to the State of Wei to realize his political aspirations. To make a breakthrough in this difficult situation and to make Duke Ling of Wei entrust him with important tasks, Confucius decided to try to persuade Duke Ling of Wei by making use of his relationship with Nan Zi. So, Confucius was eager to meet Nan Zi so as to use her as a means to persuade Duke Ling of Wei to give him an official position.

In order to meet Confucius, Nan Zi sent some people to Confucius, saying, "People from anywhere must pay a formal visit to me if they want to see the king of Wei. I am also very willing to meet wise people from every part of the country so as to broaden my knowledge."

Confucius went to the harem, where Nan Zi lived. When he arrived there, Confucius performed a standard bow to Nan Zi who was sitting behind a silk curtain. Confucius only heard the noise made by her ornaments and her soft voice. They talked for a while politely with nothing mentioned about putting Confucius in an important position in Duke Ling of Wei's government. Confucius regretted this meeting. He said to his students, "I've never had any interest in meeting such a woman. Our meeting was just a courteous one." In spite of his explanation, most of his students thought that the meeting was not necessary. Zi Lu, a frank man, said seriously, "It is a real disgrace for our teacher to meet this kind of woman. No wonder people suspect that you want to get some special favor from her." His words angered Confucius, who denied what Zi Lu said about him. "I had no other purpose or intentions. This is only a meeting between friends. What disgraceful things have I done that make me unable to be forgiven by God?"

This meeting really did Confucius no good. On the contrary, Duke Ling of Wei no longer thought of Confucius as an upright and majestic person. One day, when Duke Ling of Wei and Nan Zi were traveling on a high carriage, he asked Confucius to sit on the second carriage, on which sat one of his favorite officials named Yong Qu. As people watched the entourage traveling through the streets, they took it as big news that perhaps Duke Ling of Wei did this to demonstrate to others that he had a close relationship with Confucius. But Confucius took this as an unbearable insult to himself.

"I have never seen any person who attaches more importance to moralities than to beauties," he said angrily afterwards. His words show his dissatisfaction with Duke Ling of Wei and his travel arrangements through the main streets of town.

Duke Ling of Wei's son, Kuai Kui, hated Nan Zi as he observed Duke Ling of Wei doting on her and indulging with her all day long in debauchery. So Kuai Kui sent a man to assassinate her. Once he saw Nan Zi, however, the assassin didn't dare to carry out his mission. As Kuai Kui kept winking at him, Nan Zi realized their scheme and cried out, "Kuai Kui is going to kill me!" Hearing the shouting, Duke Ling of Wei arrived immediately, which frightened Kuai Kui away. Realizing that he could no longer stay in the State of Wei, Kuai Kui went to seek refuge with Zhao Jianzi in the State of Jin.

At the demand of Nan Zi, Duke Ling of Wei decided to dispatch his troops to the State of Jin so as to catch his son, Kuai Kui, and to bring him back to his state. He sent for Confucius and sought his advice about his fighting plan. "You didn't fight when you should fight," thought Confucius, "and now you want to fight just to please your concubine." Realizing that in this war, the relationship between the father and the son as well as that of the two states would be involved, he did not want to offend either party. So he said to Duke Ling of Wei, "If you ask me about how to worship heaven and ancestors, I will be able to offer you some help because I am an expert in this field. But now you ask me about how to fight this war, I am sorry to tell you that I know nothing about it." Of course, his answer dissatisfied Duke Ling of Wei. The next day, when they were having another talk, Duke Ling of Wei looked at the wild geese in the sky while he was answering Confucius' questions, which made Confucius sense an obvious distance from the king. So he knew it was the time for him to leave the State of Wei.

Before long, after ruling the state for 42 years, Duke Ling of Wei passed away. The struggle inside the State of Wei became more and more intense. Nan Zi wanted to enthrone his youngest son, Ying, in accordance with Duke Ling of Wei 's will. But Ying dared not to accept this because his elder brother Kuai Kui was still in the State of Jin. As a result, Nan Zi asked Duke Ling of Wei's grandson, Zhe to ascend to the throne, who was known as Duke Chu of Wei. As Kuai Kui was unwilling to accept this, he decided to return to Wei to struggle with his son for the throne with the support of Zhao Jianzi. But he and his supporters were stopped at the border by Duke Chu of Wei 's soldiers.

In Confucius' mind, neither Duke Chu of Wei's behavior nor his father's behavior was moral; the State of Jin's support for Kuai Kui was not justified; the State of Qi's help for Duke Chu of Wei was not right. It was very difficult to say who was right or wrong in such a confusing situation. Not wanting to be involved in it, Confucius made up his mind to leave the State of Wei. Before he left, he said the following words to criticize the political situation in

Wei, "The State of Lu and the State of Wei were so alike because of the troubles and the chaos aroused in them. When King Wu of the Zhou Dynasty died many years ago, Guan Shu and Cai Shu rebelled against the new king, who was put into a very difficult situation. Now in the State of Wei governed by the descendants of Kang Shu, the family members fight against each other. How miserable this is!"

Sighing by the Yellow River

Confucius came to the State of Wei with enthusiasm in the hope of carrying out his ambitions that he could not realize in the State of Lu. But he had achieved nothing through his trials and hardships in Wei. Of course, Confucius would not give up easily. But now he decided to leave Wei to find another way out. But where could he go? Once, he wanted to go to Zhongmou and at another time, he intended to go to the State of Jin.

As a family servant of Fan and Zhong Xing, two ministers of the State of Jin, Fu Xi governed Zhongmou, the fief of the family Fan and family Zhong Xing. Zhongmou was not far from the northwestern frontier of the State of Wei. In the first year of the reign of Duke Ai of Lu, that is the 41 year of the reign of Duke Ling of Wei, Zhao Yang from the State of Jin crusaded against Chao Ge, the family of Fan and the family of Zhong Xing. At the same time, Fu Xi, who was occupying Zhongmou, rebelled against the State of Jin, claiming his loyalty to the State of Wei and inviting Confucius to his land. As Confucius was eager to realize his aspiration, he wanted to leave for Zhongmou as soon as this opportunity came to him. Trying to persuade him not to go, one of his students, Zi Lu said, "I used to hear you teach us, 'A gentleman should not support someone who personally does something evil.' Now, this Fu Xi in Zhongmou is rebelling against Jin, how can you go and support him?"

"Yes," said Confucius, "It is true that I said that. But, haven't you realized that the hardest object cannot become thinner after being ground and the whitest object cannot turn black no matter how hard you try to dye it? Am I a useless bitter melon that can only be hung there?" Though Confucius in the end did not leave for Zhongmou, we can see from this incident that on the one hand, Confucius stuck to his own principles when handling matters. On the other hand, he was a very flexible person.

Visiting the State of Jin had long been the wish of Confucius because the State of Jin was a large country and Duke Wen of Jin (reigning from 636 BC to 628 BC) used to "shake the heaven and the earth" when he was ruling the State. Even in the last stage of the Spring and Autumn Period, the State of Jin was still very strong and influential. It was more meaningful to begin one's political career here than in any other state. When Confucius was taking office in the State of Lu, he was very much interested in the political situation in Jin. Then, the real ruler was a minister named Zhao Yang, but a tense struggle was going on among groups led by Han, Zhao, Wei, Zhi, Fan, and Zhong Xing. Confucius wanted very much to meet Zhao Yang so that they could make some contributions to the easing up of the tense situation and to the future development of the State of Jin. That winter, to implement his own political belief, Confucius decided to cross the Yellow River with Zi Gong and some of his other students, with the State of Jin as their destination. But, when they just got to the bank of the Yellow River before crossing the border of the State of Wei, Confucius learned that Zhao Yang had killed two virtuous people of the State of Jin, Ming Du and Dou Chou, whom Confucius held in high respect. What Zhao Yang did showed that he not only disrespected talented people, but also regarded them as his enemies. Confucius knew that he could never be linked with such a person as Zhao Yang. Gazing at the Yellow River from its bank, Confucius sighed because now he could not go west by crossing the beautiful Yellow River. Maybe this was just his fate.

Feeling confused, Zi Gong asked Confucius what they could learn from the killing of Ming Du and Dou Chou. "These two talented people," said Confucius, "helped Zhao Yang get power when he was not very successful. When he got power, Zhao Yang killed these two who had contributed so much to him. This is called 'requite kindness with enmity.' I used to hear people say, "If his babies are killed, the unicorn will not appear in the outskirts of the city; if people dry up a river so as to catch fish, the flood dragon will not send rain to this place; if her nests are destroyed, the beautiful phoenix will not arrive. Why is this? The reason is that all kinds of creatures mourn over their family members who have passed away. Even the animals and birds know this, I can be no exception."

As he was returning to the east, Confucius stopped in the Town of Zou to have a rest, where he wrote a poem to express his indignation and his great aspiration. After reciting his poem, he felt a little relieved.

Although he did not succeed in crossing the river, Confucius didn't want to come here in vain. He took this opportunity to visit the town of Pu, a place his student Zi Lu had governed for three years. When he arrived there, Confucius found that the land had been well cultivated and no wild grass could be found in the field. The houses there were also arranged in a good order and the green trees were flourishing. The yard where Zi Lu's office was located was very quiet as no one went there to cry out his grievances and to ask for the justice to be done. After seeing this, Confucius believed this resulted from Zi Lu's faithful application of his teaching to his own administration. Confucius thought this could be regarded as excellent achievement, so he complimented him again and again. Later, people referred to this incident as "giving three compliments while passing the town of Pu."

Passing the State of Song
in Plain Clothes

Confucius and his students stayed in the State of Wei for more than five years without achieving anything significant. So as soon as Confucius heard that Duke Min of Chen (who reigned from 501 BC to 479 BC) in the south respected the talented people no matter what their social position, he decided to visit the State of Chen via the States of Cao and Song. According to the recorded history, when they reached a place named Yi, a local official in charge of guarding the border said to people, "I meet everybody who is anybody who passes here." After calling on Confucius, he said to local people, "Friends, are we still afraid of the turbulent world? Since the world is now in such a mess, I believe that God has appointed Confucius to alter this situation."

It is said that when Confucius and his students reached a place near the State of Song, it suddenly started to rain. In a hurry to find shelter, Confucius and his students rushed into a cave. Later, the local people came to regard it as an honor that Confucius stayed in this cave. They carved figures in its walls, built a temple in front of the cave and in different periods erected many monuments to commemorate this incident.

It didn't take long before Confucius and his students arrived in the State of Song. Once they reached there, Confucius was lost in thoughts. This place was very dear to him because his ancestors came from the State of Song. At that time, the capital of Song was in today's Shangqiu. Before they paid a visit to the capital, Confucius and his students came to Li (Xiayi County in today's Henan Province) to the south of Shangqiu. Li was situated fifty kilometers south of Shangqiu. It was a place known for its rich products and artless folk customs. In the past, when Fu Fuhe, the ancestor of Confucius, gave up his throne to his brother Fu Si, he was appointed the governor in Li. Among his descendants Zheng Kaofu and Kong Fujia had contributed greatly to the building of the nation and its military force. According to *The Book of Rites*, Confucius said that he grew up in the State of Lu and lived in Song. Thus, Confucius did come to Song, especially to Li, where his ancestors used to live. In his later years, Confucius mentioned many times that he was "a man from Yin" because he could not forget that he was a descendant of the Emperor of Shang. He even could not give up this idea when he was considering his marriage, one of the most important events in people's life. He decided to marry a girl from his ancestor's place. As a result, a girl called Bing Guan Shi from this place became his wife. This further showed that Confucius could not forget his motherland. Later, in memory of Confucius' returning to his motherland, the local people built up temples, where the images of Confucius' ancestors, starting from Fu Fuhe, were worshipped. A thousand years later, the direct descendants of Confucius from Qufu still came to settle down here, a fact that showed their deep feeling towards their ancestors.

In view of the dramatic social changes, some people at that time could only think in the short-term without the ability to look at events from a historical perspective. Duke Jing of Song praised Confucius' theory but said he could not put his theory into practice.

Sima Huanzhui, minister of war in the State of Song and grandson of Xiang Xu who was an old minister in Song and a descendant of Duke Huan of Song, was very arrogant. Taking advantage of his power as a ranking official, he led a luxurious life. He even ordered a huge and heavy coffin that tired many workers to death in the three years it took to make it. On hearing this, Confucius felt outraged, saying, "It would be better for people living such a luxurious life to die and then rot as soon as possible."

These remarks of Confucius left a bad impression on Sima Huanzhui when he heard them, and he made up his mind to take revenge on Confucius at the first opportunity. When Confucius and his students reached the capital of Song, they would practice rites under a tree outside the western gate of the capital. They did this in accordance with the rites passed down from the Zhou Dynasty. One day, as they were doing their practice, a group of strongmen approached and ordered them to stop. Before Confucius and his students had an opportunity to speak, these men started to chop down this tree. As they were cutting down the tree, they threatened Confucius, urging him and his students to leave the State of Song, otherwise they would suffer the same fate as the tree. On seeing this crisis, the students wanted to make preparations to leave in a hurry. But Confucius remained calm. He comforted his students, "God has given me the task to pass on the ethics, what can Sima Huanzhui do to me?"

In spite of his words, Confucius still arranged for everyone to leave immediately. To avoid any persecution by Sima Huanzhui, Confucius asked his students to wear plain clothes and to leave Song in separate groups. Agreeing to meet before the city gate of Xinzheng, the capital of the State of Zheng (Xinzheng City in today's Henan Province), some students went south and some went west. Receiving a report from his strongmen, Sima Huanzhui immediately ordered them to stop Confucius and his students. But by the time they were able to act, Confucius and his students were gone.

After they escaped the capital of Song in plain clothes, Confucius and some of his students went south. After several days' difficult traveling, they reached a place just outside the State of Zheng. As the first one to reach there, Confucius waited for his students to come one by one. At the same time, his students also went around asking about the whereabouts of their teacher.

"Did you meet a person" asked Zi Gong, "whose cheeks are like those of the ancient emperor, Tang Yao; whose neck is like one of the famous ancient judges, Gao Tao; whose shoulders are like those of Zi Chan, the great statesman in the State of Zheng and whose body is like the one of Da Yu, the ancient hero who had conquered the flood?"

"I have never seen a person with all the characteristics you described," answered one man. "But I did see a confounded old man who is tall and looks like a stray dog."

Following this old man's directions, Zi Gong found Confucius. When Zi Gong related to Confucius what the old man had said, Confucius answered with a sad smile: "I don't deserve to be compared to virtuous people or saints. And I really do look like a stray dog."

The pathos in Confucius' words would seem

natural coming from a man in his sixties traveling from one place to another without a destination. He spoke as he did also because he was far away from his homeland and no one wanted to use his talent.

Confucius had been a great admirer of Zi Chan in the State of Zheng. Now that he had reached Zheng, certainly he would stay for some time there so as to do some research work. Through his investigation, he praised Zi Chan for his "four merits," which included his proper and dignified manners, his serious attitude towards the work assigned to him by the king, his method of educating people through ethics and his righteous way of handling people. The high praise that Confucius gave to Zi Chan should encourage people to learn from him.

In his life, Zi Chan set up many schools in his state, through which common people could be educated and trained. These schools could also serve as a channel to strengthen the relationship between the people and the government. The results were so satisfactory that Confucius kept complimenting the schools in Zheng and admired Zi Chan more and more.

Courteous Reception in the State of Chen and the State of Hou

After their brief meeting in the State of Zheng and after enduring all the hardships of the long journey, Confucius and his students arrived in the State of Chen (southeast of Henan Province). According to legend, people of Chen were descendants of Shun. The capital city of this small kingdom was Wanqiu (present-day Huaiyang County in Henan Province). As soon as they arrived in Chen, Confucius called on Sicheng Zhenzi, a high official, who later introduced them to Chen Mingong, the king of Chen. At that time, Chen Mingong had been king for ten years. As a virtuous and moral king, he had been admiring the moral character and the knowledge of Confucius and his students for a long time, so he was very pleased to have them in his kingdom. Treating them as honored guests, he invited them to live in the best hotel in the kingdom. In this way, Confucius and his students settled down comfortably. By then, Confucius was already sixty years old. Later, as he looked back on his whole life, he said:

"When I turned sixty, I could judge the real motive of a person by his words." In other words, Confucius was saying that when he reached sixty, his mind became more determined and his behavior more definite. He would do and say the things according to his belief and refused to agree to say or to do the things that went against his belief. When he was in the State of Chen, he thought that the King of Chen was so wise and treated him so well that he realized that the time had come for him to turn his ambitions into reality.

When he was staying in the State of Chen, now and then, Confucius asked about the situation in the State of Lu. By then, Duke Ding of Lu had died and his son succeeded to the throne as Duke Ai. In the third year of Duke Ai's reign (492 BC), Lu was struck by an earthquake. In the same year, a great fire broke out that burned down the temples of Huangong and Xigong. As a matter of fact, according to the rites of Zhou, these two temples should never have existed in the first place. Therefore, Confucius was very happy to hear this news, saying to himself, "This is the perfect punishment for those who disobey the rites of Zhou."

Chen Mingong respected Confucius so much that he regarded him as his teacher, to whom he often turned for help and advice when he had some questions. One day, a small eagle shot by an arrow dropped to the ground from the sky with the stone arrow pierced through its back. No one knew where this one-foot and eight-inch-long arrow had come from. Chen Mingong sent people to Confucius to seek his thoughts.

"This arrow," Confucius said, "was made in an ancient northern country called Sushen. When King Wu of Zhou conquered Shang Dynasty, all minority peoples came to pay in tribute to King Wu of Zhou. The gift presented by the people from Sushen was this kind of arrow. Later, the arrows were distributed to the sons and daughters of the king. The daughter of King Wu of Zhou was married to Yu Hugong, who was later assigned to govern in the State of Chen. The late king distributed these foreign gifts to those who had made great contributions to the country, including to those with the same family name as his and to those who had the different family names. He did this because he wanted these people to be loyal to him in safeguarding the territory and to show proper respect to him. If you have any doubts about this, you can go and have a look at the storeroom where these objects are kept."

Chen Mingong asked people to look and what they found did agree with Confucius' explanation. Since then, people respected Confucius more and more for his great knowledge and rich experience.

There are many examples about Confucius' erudition.

When Ji Huanzi ordered people to clean a well, the workers found a clay pot in the earth. After digging it out, they found something resembling sheep bones. How did the sheep enter the well? As no one could give a proper answer, Ji Huanzi asked people to send for Confucius. After examining the bones, Confucius offered a logical explanation:

"I have heard that the monster in wood is named Kui; the monster in stone is named Wangliang; the monster in water is named Long Guixiang and the monster in earth is named the Sheep of Fen, which looks very like a real sheep but lives under the earth. People buried these bones under the earth so as to prevent the Sheep of Fen from doing harm to people and animals."

After hearing this explanation, Ji Huanzi and others present felt that they had learned something great from Confucius.

Once, when the State of Wu seized Kuaiji (present-day Shaoxing City in Zhejiang Province), the capital city of the State of Yue, they found a cart fully loaded with big bones. They were apparently no ordinary bones. What on earth were they? As no one knew the answer, this matter was laid aside for a while. Several days later, an ambassador from the State of Wu paid a formal visit to the State of Lu. Confucius was invited to the banquet to welcome the ambassador. At the end of the banquet, the ambassador took out a bone and asked Confucius:

"We purposely brought this bone from the south. Would you please tell us what kind of bone this was? This big bone is like neither human bones nor animals bones. We have been puzzled for many years. Now, we would like to ask your favor to enlighten us. Would you mind helping us?"

After a careful look at the bone, Confucius answered: "I heard that when the great king of Yu was to ascend the throne, he sent out orders for all gods and spirits to meet at Kuaiji Mountain so as to take actions according to the order of Yu. A man with the family name of Fangfeng arrived late, so he was beheaded in accordance with the laws in the army. Later, his bones were loaded onto a cart, which were just what you had found."

"How can this Fangfeng be a god?" the ambassador asked.

"The ancient gods in charge of mountains and rivers were called gods so long as they help keep order of the land," Confucius replied. "Those who took care of the local land were granted peerages."

"Which mountain was this Fangfeng in charge of?" the ambassador asked.

"He was in charge of Mount Fengyu." Confucius answered. "His people were called Wangmang during the dynasty of Shun, Yu and Shang and they were called Changdi in the Zhou Dynasty. They were known as the 'giants' because of their large size."

Confucius' answer immediately enlightened all the people about the mystery of the bones. As a result, Confucius' reputation as a talented erudite was spread to every kingdom in China.

In the third year of the reign of Duke Ai of the State of Lu (492 BC), Ji Huanzi, who had ruled the kingdom for many years became seriously ill. When he was traveling in his cart passing through the State of Lu, he remembered Confucius, who had advised him to demolish the city wall.

"Our kingdom should be able to flourish," he sighed, "The kingdom did not become strong because we offended such talented people as Confucius so that we have no talents to govern the kingdom." Turning his head, he said to his successor, Ji Kangzi: "It seems that you will succeed to the throne after my death. When you are ruling the state, you should try your best to ask Confucius and his students to come back to the State of Lu because they all have skills to rule the country."

Before long, Ji Huanzi died and Ji Kangzi came to the throne and began to rule the state in place of his father. After burying his father, he had the idea of inviting Confucius back. However, Confucius left the State of Lu because of the opposition from various kinds of people. As a result, it was not enough for Ji Kangzi to change his opinion about Confucius. Since many people were against inviting Confucius to the State of Lu, Ji Kangzi decided to first call on Confucius' students such as Zi Gong and Ran Qiu.

As a small country with a limited population, the military strength of the State of Lu was weak. As a result, it was often bullied by other state. In 488 BC, the State of Wu in the south forced the State of Lu to meet in Zengcheng City to discuss forming an alliance between the two states. The State of Wu asked Lu to present 100 pigs, sheep and cattle to it as articles of tribute. In addition, a minister of Wu named Bo Pi ordered Ji Kangzi to personally call on him. As he was afraid of the military power of Wu, Ji Kangzi did not dare to refuse. Fortunately, he asked Zi Gong, one of Confucius' students to go with him in a hurry, which kept him from being seriously insulted. The diplomatic failure made Ji Kangzi more anxious to have more wise and ingenious people to help him. Therefore, he made up his mind to invite another student of Confucius', Ran Qiu back to his kingdom.

In response to Ji Kangzi's invitation, Ran Qiu decided to return to the State of Lu. Before he left Confucius, Confucius encouraged him sincerely and meaningfully, which also showed Confucius' homesickness. Zi Gong, who had just returned from his mission as a diplomat for the State of Lu, understood Confucius very well. So he admonished Ran Qiu by saying, "In the future, when you are appointed to a high position, please don't forget to take our teacher along." Ran Qiu nodded in an understanding way.

After saying good-bye to the teacher, Ran Qiu left for the State of Lu to take office. Confucius, on the other hand, stayed in the State of Chen for another three years. Among the states he had traveled through, the State of Chen under Chen Mingong was the only one that treated him well and respected him. Accordingly, Confucius should have been able to use his knowledge and skills in this state so as to realize his aspiration. But, the State of Chen was often assaulted by two larger states, the State of Jin and the State of Chu because it was sandwiched between the two. And because of this, the king of Chen had little real power, and his proposals were often rejected by force. Although Chen Mingong gave Confucius royal treatment, Confucius still thought that this kingdom was not the place in which he wanted to stay for a long time because here he could not put his talent into full play. So he said to his students, "Let's go back! Let's go back! You have great ambitions and you should go to places where these ambitions can be realized." So he thanked Chen Mingong and left for the State of Cai, followed by his students.

Like the State of Chen, the State of Cai was also a small kingdom, which was located along the southeast of Chen in today's Shangcai County in Henan Province. The State of Cai was in the same boat as the State of Chen. Having no other alternatives, Confucius and his students once again had to leave for the State of Chu.

Meeting Hermits on the Way to the State of Chu

Throughout his whole life Confucius' doctrine was to try his best to put the world in good order by actively involving himself in world affairs. Seeing a world in chaos, Confucius made up his mind to make every effort to change this situation. He had a whole set of excellent principles for governing the country and a set of effective methods for implementing them. When he took office in the State of Lu, he did make some achievements and his skills were put to use. When he was forced out of the State of Lu, or rather, when he left the state on his own accord, he decided to go to other states to find more opportunities to be a governor. And in this way, he hoped to realize his ambitions. But, it had never occurred to him that in a time when the system of rites and music was destroyed and the whole world was undergoing reform and turbulence, his traditional principles could not be applied.

Wherever Confucius went, his opinions and proposals were rejected. Some people did treat him in a friendly way, but only for the sake of appearance.

Some listened to his proposals, but mainly to make themselves feel comfortable. In spite of every opposition, Confucius did not give up his belief and his effort in implementing his principles. He unswervingly kept up his lobbying in many states. Meanwhile, over the years many people laughed at and ridiculed Confucius and his students in a way that demonstrates the level of disapproval and opposition at the time to their propositions and actions. The examples given below could help us understand this better:

Confucius and his students were traveling towards the State of Cai when they lost their way. Confucius asked Zi Lu, his student, to find the way. Very politely, Zi Lu asked two farmers who were plowing the field side by side where the ferry crossing was. These two farmers, Chang Ju and Jie Ni asked Zi Lu slowly, "Who is sitting in that cart?"

"Confucius," Zi Lu answered.

"Is he the Confucius from the State of Lu?" they asked in a rude manner.

"Yes, he is," Zi Lu answered.

The older farmer named Chang Ju smiled with contempt, saying: "He should have known the place of ferry crossing a long time ago." What he said was a pun in Chinese. What he really meant was that since Confucius knew how to live a good life, he shouldn't have to ask others about where to go. Zi Lu was really offended, but he could not find a way to express his anger. Just then, the younger farmer, Jie Ni, asked him: "Who are you?"

"I am Zhong You," answered Zi Lu.

"So you are the student of Confucius," said the farmer.

"Yes, I am. So what?" said Zi Lu angrily.

Shaking his head, he rebuked Zi Lu: "Evil people and evil deeds today fill the world just like a flood. How can people like you change this kind of situation? Even if you have reformed one place, how can you be certain that evils will not appear again in another place? In my opinion, you'd better stop asking for trouble. It is better for you to follow us so as to escape from this whole society than to follow Confucius to change the society and to escape from the evil?"

With these words, the two farmers went back to their work without paying any more attention to Zi Lu.

The surprising words from these two men left Zi Lu speechless. Since he could not answer back, Zi Lu reported this to Confucius exactly as it happened. Actually, Confucius had already overheard everything they talked about. After hearing Zi Lu's account, Confucius said:

"It is true that we can meet all kinds of unusual people and all kinds of strange things in this big world. I never had realized that there exist people who are so indifferent to what is going on around them. Since we cannot coexist peacefully with beasts and birds, with whom can we communicate if we stop our contact with other people? Just because this world is now in a chaotic state, it is up to us to change it. If peace had already been found in this world, do we still need to reform it?"

What Confucius said reflected his belief in keeping the world order and demonstrated his disagreement with Chang Ju and Jie Ni on this issue. In this way, his students learned a good lesson from him.

Several days later, Zi Lu again lagged behind when he was walking with Confucius. This time, he met another strange person, an elderly man carrying his hoe on his walking stick.

"Did you see our teacher, Confucius?" Zi Lu asked him.

Blinking his eyes, the old man answered, "Who is your teacher but a lazy man who cannot distinguish different grains?"

With these words, he continued his walk without paying further attention to Zi Lu. His impolite answer irritated Zi Lu, who realized from his words that his teacher was not far away from him. So he hurried his steps and caught up with Confucius, to whom he related this incident.

"This elderly man," said Confucius, "is a hermit. Let's go find him and ask his opinion about governing the state." But when they went to look for him, the old man had already gone.

During the Spring and Autumn Period, there existed in the society such hermits as Chang Ju and Jie Ni, who were very dissatisfied with the current chaotic society, in which the subjects rebelled against their ruler and the humble people bullied the nobles. Since these hermits had no way to prevent this from happening, they decided to give a passive response by escaping from the world. When they could no longer see or hear what was going on around them, they had peace in their hearts by escaping from a harsh reality that they could not change. Actually, this was an irresponsible attitude in dealing with world affairs. By contrast, Confucius and his students took up a positive attitude towards all things, and they played an active role in getting people involved in societal affairs. Although they could not succeed, they decided to work till the very end. They worked to carry out what they believed to be true. This is a very important characteristic of Confucianism.

Almost at the same time, another incident happened to Confucius. One day, a maniac from the State of Chu approached Confucius' cart wearing ragged clothes and with his hair disheveled. While he was walking, he was humming a song:

> *Oh! Phoenix!*
> *How have you become so confounded?*
> *Let unhappy bygones be bygones,*
> *As you can still try your best to make a future.*
> *Let it be! Let it be!*
> *How many officials in power are nice ones?*

Confucius was very surprised at these words. He wanted to get off the carriage to have a talk with the man. But this man left without paying Confucius any regard. Thinking this over for a long time, Confucius realized that he should be able to distinguish different governors. He should follow those who would like to seek his advice and leave alone those who refused to listen to him. He believed that to realize his political ambition, he should learn to take lessons from his failures as well as to have a strong determination. In addition, a flexible strategy was necessary. It was really difficult to take the responsibility of governing a country in a chaotic state. But, the more difficult task was still waiting for him.

Food Supply Cut off in the States of Chen and Cai

As Confucius and his students were traveling towards the State of Chu after they had left the State of Chen and the State of Cai, a most unhappy thing happened to them.

In the sixth year of the reign of Duke Ai of Lu (489 BC), the State of Wu initiated an attack against the State of Chen. To fight against the enemy in the east — the State of Wu — the State of Chu sent its army to Chengfu to help the State of Chen. According to the historical records, when Duke Zhao of Chu heard that Confucius and his students were traveling between the State of Chen and the State of Cai, he wanted to send for Confucius. When the news got around, some ministers in Chen and Cai advised their King:

"Confucius is a wise and talented man with many skills. If he is appointed to a position in the State of Chu, the small states like ours will be in danger."

Accordingly, some people were sent from the two states to besiege Confucius and his students in the wilderness between the State of Chen and the

State of Cai. As a result, Confucius and his students found themselves blocked from going any further although they did not know why.

Confucius, who was always moving from one place to another, found it impossible to return to his own homeland. What's worse was that he was under siege. For seven days, Confucius and his entourage could not make a fire to cook anything to eat, so they were distressed and hungry. Some became sick because of the unfavorable living conditions. The demanding circumstances offered a real challenge to all of them, especially to Confucius.

Even so, such severe conditions left Confucius as determined as usual with no inclination to change his mind. Although the people besieging them were shouting and their horses were neighing and his students were complaining with great anger — Confucius kept on teaching, reciting poems, playing his harp and singing. Most of his students could not concentrate on his teaching. One of them, Zi Lu, a hothead, said: "You often tell us that we are gentlemen. How can a gentleman be so helpless and miserable?"

Slowly and calmly, Confucius replied: "A gentleman with a lofty morality should stick to his own belief unswervingly even in very miserable situations. By contrast, a mean person will do anything after being forced into a difficult situation."

From this, we can know that Confucius could

use his strong spiritual beliefs to support himself and empower himself.

Although Confucius tried to comfort his students with these words, his students still had a lot of complaints in this kind of unstable situation. To calm his students down, he began asking them questions. Firstly, he told Zi Lu to come forward and asked him: "Do you remember an ancient poem, which says

Not a rhinoceros, not a tiger,
But why does he wander in the desert?"

Confucius continued, asking Zi Lu, "Is what we advocate correct? Or are we in such a difficult situation simply because our beliefs and principles are wrong?"

Without thinking, Zi Lu posited: "Perhaps it is because we are not virtuous, wise or tactful enough that people refuse to carry out our principles."

Of course, Confucius strongly disagreed with this answer and said Zi Lu lacked some moral and ethic principles. Then using the same poem, Confucius put the same question to Zi Gong. Zi Gong answered:

"I believe that our teacher's belief is too lofty for people to accept. In my opinion, maybe our teacher should lower his standards a little bit."

Again, Confucius criticized Zi Gong, saying: "Your ambition is somewhat too small."

Zi Gong returned to his place after being criticized. When Yan Hui came forward, Confucius recited that poem for the third time, and asked him this question: "Perhaps our beliefs and principles are not correct. That's why we are besieged here by so many people." As his favorite student, Yan Hui was well known for his wisdom, morality and wit. His answer was:

"It is true that your ideas as a teacher are too lofty for people to accept. But with some efforts you can turn the ideal into reality. It really matters little whether people accept the ideas or not. The more doubt they have of our beliefs, the more knowledgeable and educated we appear. It is our shame if we cannot present good principles. But it is a shame for people in power who cannot put these good principles into practice. It really doesn't matter much if others cannot accept our beliefs. The more difficulty people have in accepting our principles, the more obvious we appear as gentlemen."

Yan Hui spoke out what was deep in Confucius' heart. Hearing this, Confucius shouted with excitement: "You are perfect, Yan Hui. You are really an excellent boy with great skills and knowledge. If you become rich one day, I am going to help you keep your accounts."

It is said that after seven days, Confucius and his students still could not start a fire to cook a meal. With great difficulties, they found a little rice — barely enough to cook some porridge for everyone. Confucius asked his favorite student, Yan Hui to do this. Many of the students were eagerly waiting to have some porridge. Suddenly, Zi Gong saw Yan Hui, who was cooking near the pot, help himself to a spoonful of porridge behind everyone's back. Immediately, Zi Gong reported this to Confucius, saying, "How can a benevolent and virtuous gentleman do such an immoral thing?"

"If he is really a benevolent and virtuous person," answered Confucius, "He should never do such an immoral thing."

"Your favorite student," continued Zi Gong, "took the advantage of cooking and helped himself to some porridge. How can you account for this?" Confucius was dumbfounded after hearing this. On the one hand, he trusted Yan Hui's integrity. But, on the other hand, he could not ignore what Zi Gong had told him. What should he do? He found a good way to look into this.

When Yan Hui finished cooking and everyone was ready to share the food, Confucius said to his students, "I had a dream last night, in which I saw our late king. He asked us to sacrifice some food to him before we start eating. But he wanted only clean food. Is the porridge in the pot clean?"

Before Confucius could finish, Yan Hui answered immediately, "Of course it is clean. Just now, when I was cooking, something dirty from the ceiling fell into the pot. In a hurry, I fetched it out with the spoon. I had thought of throwing it away, but I realized it was a waste to drop the rice in the spoon. So, while holding the cover of the pot in one hand, I sucked out the dirt from the spoon in the other hand with my mouth, and then I put the porridge left in the spoon into the pot. So, the porridge in the pot is clean and can be sacrificed to the late king."

In an instant, Confucius was enlightened by this answer. Zi Gong also realized that he wrongly blamed Yan Hui and felt sorry for him. From this, he learnt a lesson that he should not jump to conclusions arbitrarily.

When Confucius and his students were besieged, on the one hand, he tried to calm his students with comforting words. On the other hand, he sent the eloquent Zi Gong to the State of Chu, asking Duke Zhao of Chu to dispatch an army contingent to help them out. Duke Zhao of Chu immediately agreed to this and sent his army to rescue them. With the protection of the army from Chu, Confucius and his students reached Fuhan (today's Xinyang City in Henan Province) in the State of Chu.

Touring Through the State of Chu

After they were rescued, Confucius and his students reached Fuhan in the State of Chu.

On their way to Fuhan, they passed a place named Ye (south of the County of Ye in Henan Province), which was a territory of Chu. The governor there was a minister named Shen Zhuliang, whom people respectfully called General Ye. On seeing Confucius' arrival, he went to seek his advice on being a good governor.

"Someone can be called a good governor," answered Confucius, "when people from afar submit to his authority." Several days later, General Ye asked Zi Lu, "What is your teacher like?" Zi Lu found it difficult to give a correct answer. After hearing this, Confucius said to Zi Lu, "Why didn't you tell him that your teacher is a man who works so hard that he neglects his meal and who is so excited about his study that he forgets his sorrow? He works so hard that he has grown old before he realizes it." In this way, Confucius describes himself as a person who works tirelessly and who finds great joy in learning. This was a true description of himself; he really was such a man.

Another time, General Ye told Confucius about an upright man in his hometown who informed against his father who had stolen a sheep. "Isn't this kind of son upright since he had the courage to accuse his own father?" He asked. Confucius answered, "People in my hometown looked at this matter differently. They believe that a son should help conceal a father's guilt and the father, the son's guilt. If people do this, they are thought to be righteous." Confucius said this to emphasize the importance of filial piety, which was a very important element in the traditional concept of family at that time. But he went to such an extreme that he turned the truth upside down. Obviously what he said here was very wrong.

Through all kinds of difficulties and hardships, Confucius and his students reached the State of Chu (an area in today's Hubei and Hunan provinces). Duke Zhao of Chu intended to have Confucius as his advisor. In return, he decided to give a large piece of land to Confucius as reward. But the nobles opposed this idea. As their representative, Yin Zixi said, "All those students of Confucius are outstanding, let alone Confucius himself. Which diplomat traveling through the states can do better than Zi Gong? Who can compare himself with Yan Hui in terms of governing the nation and assessing the governor with virtue and morality? In terms of leading an army to fight in the front or to defend the state, who can do better than Zi Lu? Can you find a better person than Zai Yu when it comes to the conducting of state affairs and the governing of the country? No people of comparable talent can be found in our state. So if Confucius and his students come here, they will exclude our nobles from the government and will also threaten the throne of our king." Hearing Yin Zixi's words, Duke Zhao of Chu gave up the idea of giving Confucius a high position and a large piece of land.

In the State of Chu, although Confucius did not achieve any great success, he spent a lot of time visiting people of different backgrounds. Many stories have been handed down to us about Confucius' life at this time. The following are just a few of them.

One day, Confucius and his students were passing through a large forest. Sitting in a cart while facing backward, Confucius noticed an elderly hunchback trying to catch cicadas by using glue on top of his bamboo pole. Wherever his pole went, cicadas were caught. Very skillfully, this old man caught many cicadas with great ease as if he were picking up something from the ground. Confucius was amazed at his skill, so he asked his student to stop the cart. Hurrying into the forest, he wanted to know how this old man had become so skillful.

As he was nearing the old man, Confucius praised

him, saying, "How skillful you are! Would you please tell me how you could become so proficient in doing this?"

"This is only a small trick," answered the old man slowly and calmly, "but to do this also requires a lot of practice. It took me about five or six months to learn this skill. At first, I put two small balls on top of the pole and tried my best to keep the balls from falling off. When I succeeded in doing that, the chances of failing to catch the cicadas became few. When I could do the same thing with three balls on top of the pole, the chances of failing became less than ten percent. As soon as I could do it with five balls, I could catch the cicadas as easily as picking up something from the ground." After a short pause, the old man continued, "When I stand here, I become motionless just like a stump. When I reach out my arm, it is as still as a branch on a tree. No matter how big this world is, no matter how many things there are, I have nothing in my heart but the wings of the cicada that I am going to catch. When I am ready to catch it, I keep my body straight. Holding my breath and opening my eyes wide, I pay attention only to the cicada in this large world. With such concentration, how can I fail to accomplish my goal with great skill?"

Hearing this, Confucius was enlightened. Immediately turning to his students, he said, "You should remember this. Whatever you do, if you can focus all your attention and strength on it, you will surely succeed. The skills that the old man has mastered can be learned by anyone through practice. The most important thing is concentration."

Another story is told about Confucius who one day reached a place named Canglang with his disciples. Here they saw a man washing his hat on the upper reach of a small stream and another man was washing his feet on the lower reach of the same stream. One of his students asked him, "Why do people use the water from the same stream for different purposes?" "Listen!" said Confucius, "What is that child singing? 'The clean water from the stream of Canglang can wash my hat and the dirty water from this stream can wash my feet.' That is, the clean and dirty can be compared to a person's character. People respect those who are self-reliant and independent, but look down upon those who insult themselves and corrupt their own reputation. From this story, we should realize that a person should respect and love himself."

Another time Confucius and his students passed a beautiful place named Agu, where the rivers were clear and the mountains were elegant. When Confucius saw a young lady with a jade ornament in her hair who was washing clothes by the river, he asked Zi Gong to test her virtue so as to discover the folkways of the local public. Taking out a wine pot, Zi Gong asked her to fill the pot with some water.

She filled the pot and put it on the shore. Again, Zi Gong took out a harp and invited her to play music. She refused. With some frivolous words, Zi Gong offered her some silk products as a gift. "As a passerby, you are so impossible," this lady said with a stern face. "I am still a young lady, so how can I accept your gift? You'd better hurry away now or my husband who is watching me in secret will give you a good punishment." After Zi Gong reported to Confucius this lady's behavior, he was very satisfied, and kept on praising the state as a place full of people who knew good manners and etiquette.

During this period of time, Confucius also fell ill occasionally. Once he was seriously sick. Everyone got nervous, then started to panic. Zi Lu, who had a very close relationship with Confucius, suggested that everyone pray to God for the teacher's recovery. After a while, Confucius came to himself. When he heard that everyone was talking about praying for him, he asked Zi Lu whether they were really going to pray. Zi Lu told him that they had thought about doing so. Knowing that Confucius had never mentioned ghosts, superior forces, evil spirits and gods, Zi Lu quoted an ancient saying to suggest to Confucius that according to the old custom, praying to gods was an acceptable practice. Confucius did not encourage people to pray for him, nor did he enjoy arguing with his students about ghosts while he was sick. So he told them that he had already prayed for himself and it was unnecessary for them to pray for him again.

Several days later, there was a little improvement in the condition of Confucius' health. When he learned that during the time of his sickness, many of his students disguised themselves as his family servants, Confucius got very angry.

"According to my social status," said Confucius, "I should not have any family servants. How can you have become so bold as to deceive the people and gods? I'd rather die in my students' care than in the care of family servants. I may not have a grand funeral after I die, but I am not going to die on the road like this."

From this, we can see clearly that Confucius did not believe in ghosts or gods and showed no interests in showing himself off in spite of his sickness. This went hand in hand with his beliefs.

Returning to the State of Wei

During his stay in the State of Chu, Confucius encountered many difficulties and hardships. He and his students spent several years looking into the society, and in doing so, they discovered some life philosophy, which was really a gain for them. But as for his main purpose — i.e. realizing his ambition in a state — it had not been realized. His future became more and more perilous. As he could not realize his ideal, he made up his mind to go to the north. In the tenth year of the reign of Duke Ai of Lu (485 BC), Confucius and his students crossed the northwest border of the State of Song, heading to the State of Wei.

On their way, they reached a place called Yi. The officer guarding this place met the students of Confucius and told them, "I have never missed any chance to meet gentlemen passing our border. Since your teacher is a talented and kind-hearted gentleman, I will try every means to call on him." Since this man spoke with such sincerity and respect, Confucius agreed to meet him because he himself also enjoyed making friends with virtuous people who loved learning. When they met each other, they had a very agreeable conversation. They regretted that they had not met each other much earlier. After this meeting, this officer said to Confucius' students, "Since you have learned so many skills and so much knowledge from Confucius, you needn't worry about finding an office for yourselves. It has been a long time since the world functioned in good order. God just wants to use your teacher as an example to wake up the world." What he actually meant was that the students would really achieve something great in the future by following their teacher.

From Yi, Confucius and his students went back to the State of Wei after passing Puyi, a city located in the south border of Wei, from which, they went north and soon reached the capital city of Wei – Diqiu (today's Puyang City in Henan Province).

At this time, the king of Wei was Duke Chu named Zhe. Many years earlier as he was getting ready to ascend to the throne, he had a fierce struggle with his father, Kuai Kui. Later, because of intense fights within different fractions in the State of Jin, Kuai Kui was not able to return to Wei to succeed to the throne. As a result, Duke Chu of Wei kept the situation in Wei stable. In the fifth and seventh year of the reign of Duke Ai of Lu, the State of Jin initiated two small-scale attacks against Wei. With the help of Kong Yu (Kong Wenzi), Zhu

Ta and Wang Sungu — all of whom in Confucius' eyes were talented people — situation in the State of Wei was stable.

Thus, when Confucius entered Wei for the second time, on the one hand, he was quite satisfied with the peace found there. On the other hand, he missed his old friends such as Duke Ling of Wei and the talented adviser, Ju Boyu. After he had settled down in a hotel, it happened that the hotel owner was holding a funeral. Getting off his cart, Confucius joined the mourning and couldn't help weeping for this family. When Confucius left the hotel, he also gave his old horse to this family. His students thought that what he did was too extreme. But Confucius answered, "I only cried for this poor family. This scene reminded me of what happened to me here several years ago, so I couldn't help weeping."

At that time, many of Confucius' students were assuming office in the State of Wei. So when they heard that Confucius had arrived, they all went to him for advice. Naturally, Duke Chu of Wei also invited this sainted elderly man to take part in many political activities. Confucius already had many a well thought out plan in his heart, which can be seen from this conversation with Zi Lu:

"What is the first thing that you are going to do if the King of Wei asks you to participate in politics?" Zi Lu asked Confucius. Confucius was extremely dissatisfied with Duke Chu's action of keeping his father out of the state. In his opinion, what he did broke the proper relations between the king and the governed as well as the relations between the father and the son. So, he took this as an opportunity to develop his theory of "justifying the name." So he answered, "I will first justify the name of the king." This bold and abrupt answer left Zi Lu confused. "Teacher," he said, "You are a little pedantic. What can you justify?"

This enraged Confucius who thought Zi Lu's response was arbitrary and showed no appreciation of his feeling. He said immediately, "Your words are too rude. Listen to me, Zhong You. A true gentleman will offer no opinion related to what he does not know. What I mean is that if the name is not justified, what a person says makes no sense. This explains Duke Chu's failure in dealing with such government affairs as manners and music. When this happens, no slave can receive a fair punishment. When the issue of manners and music cannot be handled well in a state and fair punishment cannot be carried out in this state — common people live every day in a state of uncertainty, worrying about what kind of life they should live. So, a true gentleman should find good reasons for naming a thing or using a word, that is, he should do everything in a proper way."

Thus, Confucius believed that this rule applied

not only to the relation between people but the relation between objects and their shapes. When he observed that a certain container had been made in a different form, he sighed, "This *Gu* (a kind of wine vessel) should no longer be called a *Gu*." He was showing his indignation at the fact that people disobeyed the rule passed down from the ancient times in making this *Gu*.

Confucius' belief of "justifying the name" reveals to us that in the later years of the Spring and Autumn Period the society was in a contant state of turmoil and the slavery system was on the brink of collapse. Norms and conventions were not observed. Sticking to his traditional ideas, Confucius showed his disagreement towards some changes in the society, but what he could do was only fight against it by seeking help from public opinion.

Because he was so dissatisfied with the politics in the State of Wei, Confucius refrained from intervening in political affairs. Instead, he devoted himself to cultural development. As early as when he was besieged in Kuang of Wei, he used to say, "After the death of King Wen of Zhou Dynasty, all the cultural heritages of human beings were left to us, weren't they? If God wanted to destroy these heritages, he would not have put them into our hands; if he doesn't want to eradicate these heritages, what can Kuang people do to us?"

Confucius himself claimed to be the one who

was the main heir to all the culture of human beings. Since he did not take part in public affairs, he had many things to do in cultural development. He decided to collate such ancient classics as *The Book of Songs, Collection of Ancient Texts, The Book of Rites* and *The Book of Music* to pass them down to later generations. In his early years, he was not able to collect many materials, but in his later years, he tried his best to do research and record the manners, traditions and conventions among common people. In addition, he sent his students to study conventional customs and the manners of the nobles and to report to him their findings when they returned.

By the time when Confucius was ready to leave the State of Wei for the State of Lu, he had already gained a very good understanding of the music of the common people and nobles. After he had fully appreciated and mastered the music, he made many plans on collating and reforming it so as to preserve the best of them. So, before he left the State of Wei for Lu, he became more and more active in collating all these materials.

Not long after Confucius had reached the State of Wei, his student Ran Qiu became the second student after Zi Gong to be called to the State of Lu to take office. When he returned to Lu, he was appointed the general manager of Ji Kangzi. Before long, Ran Qiu helped Ji Kangzi fight a good fight.

In the 11th year of the reign of Duke Ai of Lu

(484 BC), the State of Qi sent an army to attack the State of Lu. Leading his army on the right wing, Mengsun Fan cooperated with Ran Qiu, the left wing. They fought the Qi army in the north of city of Lu. When the battle started, because of the inept leadership of Mengsun Fan, the army of Lu was seriously defeated. The army on the left wing, with Ran Qiu as their commander, on the other hand, fought bravely and won one victory after another. Another student of Confucius, Fan Chi, wielding his spear, fought in the front and won the battle.

In a ceremony to celebrate the victory, Ji Kangzi highly praised Ran Qiu's skill in fighting. Then, he asked Ran Qiu from whom he learned these skills. Ran Qiu said that he learned them from Confucius. Ji Kangzi then asked him how Confucius was doing. Ran Qiu took this opportunity to sing the high praises of his teacher, advising the king to invite his teacher back.

The State of Lu won the battle against the State of Qi. Two things made Confucius very happy about this. Firstly, he was happy because his motherland won the war. In addition, he was glad because it was his students who led the army to gain the victory. His students put their skills into full play and gained glory for himself. So, he couldn't help getting excited. He praised Ran Qiu and Fan Chi's leading the army to fight with spears as righteous actions. He gave special acknowledgements to Wang

Qi, who was still a boy when he volunteered to go to the war when the State of Lu was in trouble. At first, people dismissed him. But, after Wang Qi explained his theory of fighting and showed his skill in fighting, the king of Lu came to highly value his skills and he ordered Wang Qi to drive a chariot like an adult. His bravery in fighting didn't disappoint. After killing and injuring many enemies, he died with his fellow soldiers because they were outnumbered.

When the war was over, people put Wang Qi's body in a coffin and wanted to hold a funeral for him appropriate for a child according to the rites of Zhou Dynasty. When Confucius heard this, he disagreed: "Although he was a child, Wang Qi took weapons to defend his nation when it was in danger. His action was the actions of an adult. So he should be buried as an adult." What Confucius said here was instructive to people because he advocated patriotism.

Meanwhile, the ruler of Lu, Ji Kangzi, sent three ministers as envoys to invite Confucius back. Gong Hua, Gong Bin and Gong Lin took gifts to invite Confucius, who was very willing to come back because his long aspiration had finally been realized. Accompanied by his students, he went back to the State of Lu with excitement and without any hesitation, thus ending a 14 years' journey through many states. By then Confucius was already 68.

On his way to the State of Lu, Confucius thought a lot about those 14 years. What remained in his mind were mostly scenes where his political views were discounted. But, during those years, he met many people of different status, which opened his eyes and gave him some comfort. As he was thinking about this in his carriage, he saw an orchid growing in the valley on the roadside. Thinking for a while, he chanted a poem on orchid to express his ambition. The main idea of this poem is this: "The wind in the valley brought the unpredictable cloudy weather. I, who have been wandering for a long time am ready to go back. The host saw me off at the outskirts of the city. Why is God so unfair to make me homeless for so many years? Where is my home in such a vast China? In this world, many people are still so foolish that they cannot recognize talented people. Although I am very old now, I still stick to my beliefs."

Confucius equates himself with the orchid to show his ethical, moral, upright and lofty character. In the past, he had been such a person; he was still such a person and he planned to be such a person in the future. As he was thinking about this, he entered the State of Lu.

Loving People and Saving Money

In 484 BC, that is, the 10th year under the reign of Duke Ai of Lu, Ji Kangzi sent his men to invite Confucius and his students back to the state. They had been to 14 states like Wei, Song, Zheng, Chen, Cai, Chu, etc., experiencing much hardship and the awkwardness of being turned down. In these places, although they didn't realize their political ambitions, they had opportunities to know different classes of people in each country, gaining more experiences and knowledge about society. At the same time, Confucius seized every opportunity possible to teach and train his students in various ways. Time was far from having been wasted.

Many people in the State of Lu came to welcome Confucius and his students upon their return, including the king himself and Ji Kangzi. Not long before, Lu had defeated the State of Qi in the battlefield. The return of Confucius added more happiness to the whole state. After spending many years in other states, Confucius and his students, now too, were overjoyed in their reunion with their families. Unfortunately, Confucius' wife died before he returned to his hometown. Their departure of more than ten years earlier became their final farewell. When Confucius returned to his home, he saw nothing had changed in the house or the yard after all those years. The three junipers, which he had planted, had grown to be very big. Seeing that everything remained the same but that his wife was no longer there, Confucius couldn't help sighing with emotion.

After Confucius returned, Ji Kangzi, who was in power at that time, respected him as the Senior Counselor of the State (retired Dafu, a senior official), intending to ensure his own position with the help of Confucius' fame. As for Confucius, now with no particular political matters to worry about, but this high position to enjoy, he employed this opportunity to advocate his principles of loving people, carrying out benevolence, exercising self-restraint and returning to propriety. On some matters, he expounded his notions more specifically. For instance, not long after his return, Ji Kangzi sent Ran Qiu to consult him about the farming tax. The farming tax was a tax collected according to the area of land farmed by every family to support the army. By this means, the newly emerged class of landlords could gain more power in the state while the system of slavery could be further damaged. Confucius had no interest in this, therefore, didn't answer the question at all. In response to Ran Qiu's insistence, he answered him in a critical tone: "A gentleman needs to follow the regulations of the Zhou Dynasty in his actions. Otherwise, even if a new tax were adopted, it would not satisfy his endless desire. If the family of Ji intended to follow the rule, he could follow the regulations of the Zhou Dynasty without consulting me. If he doesn't want to obey the rule, there is no need to ask for my opinion."

Confucius thought that a state needed to be managed with the policy of benevolence, that is, some regulations should be instituted which could protect the interests of the ruling class, strengthen the state, and at the same time allow the survival of those who are ruled. Only in this way, could long-term exploitation and control be ensured. In his opinion, benevolent policies need to be carried out as beneficial to the support of the people, and justice needs to be considered while employing people's labor. When people are engaged in farm work, it is better not to use them as laborers. Therefore, appropriate use of time should be considered in the use of people. The ruling class should economize and prevent waste to avoid excessively exploiting the people. One day, the king asked You Ruo, a student of Confucius, for his opinion.

"This year the harvest is not good and the income is not enough. What should I do?"

You Ruo answered, "Just collect one tenth of

the tax."

"In my opinion, two tenths are not enough, not to mention one tenth," said the king.

You Ruo replied with the tone of Confucius: "If the people are rich, how can their king be poor? If the people are poor, how can the king be rich?"

If the masses were rich, their ruler naturally would be wealthy. On the contrary, if the masses were poor, where would the king go for resources?

After Ran Qiu returned to the State of Lu, he became the housekeeper for the family of Ji, helping them exploit the common people. As a result, the family accumulated much wealth and became richer and richer. They also had imposed the farming tax, a new means of exploitation to collect more taxes. Confucius felt very angry at it. He said to the other students seriously, "Ran Qiu can hardly be called my student. Denounce and criticize him as much as you like."

Based on the principle of benevolence, Confucius argued against excessive exploitation, which is right. However, when Ran Qiu helped the family of Ji to collect more money, a new means of exploitation came into being. This means, based on more fortune being produced, was close to the exploitation method in a feudalistic society, and reflected a newly formed production relationship at that time. Confucius could not see this point. Observed from this perspective, his view was, to some degree, useless and not right. In 483 BC, farming tax was officially adopted in the State of Lu.

To expand his power, Ji Kangzi intended to send troops to suppress a small state nearby called Zhuanyu. Immediately, Ran Qiu and Zi Lu reported this news to their teacher. Hearing the news, Confucius criticized them and then elaborated on his views of "equalizing the fortune." He understood the conflict existing between wealth and poverty. In his opinion, if the fortunes were equalized among people, then there would be no rich people or poor people. Obviously this idea had the tendency of controlling the development of private economy, and therefore was detrimental to the development of society. But his love for and concern about the people have positive significance. His idea that the imbalance of fortune would cause social conflicts is indication that his opinions on economics were to serve his political principles.

Talking About Justice in Political Affairs

The economic principles of Confucius were to develop production and to care for the people, while his political principles were to govern with benevolence and virtue. From 483 BC, the 12th year under the reign of Duke Ai of Lu, the state suffered from calamities of locusts, drought, and famine for four years. In addition, the family of Ji increased their exploitation of the masses. Common people could barely survive, and robbery became not uncommon. Ji Kangzi was troubled by the problem of robbery. One day he asked Confucius for advice on how to solve this problem. Confucius, being more concerned about Ji Kangzi's exploitation of the people, answered directly, "Common people would not turn to robbery even under your encouragement if you were not so greedy."

Ji Kangzi planned to kill those who disturbed the order of his rule. He consulted Confucius, "Would it do if I have the bad men killed while at the same time become close to the good ones?"

"There is no need to kill. People will become

obedient if you are benevolent," said Confucius. He advised Ji Kangzi that if he behaved properly, so would the common people. Confucius continued, "The morality of the noble is like the wind, while that of the common people is the grass, moving this way or that way. It is better for the wind to stop blowing the grass." Certainly the common people would be influenced by the behavior of the ruling class. Whether a country could be well managed depended on how the rulers set examples and led the people.

Once Ji Kangzi asked Confucius, "If I want the people to be serious and careful with everything, try their best in their work, and encourage each other, what should I do?"

Confucius answered, "If you are serious about their lives, they will be serious with your orders. If you are filial to your parents and if you protect the young, they will be faithful to you. If you promote the qualified and educate the inferior, they too will become diligent."

In the State of Lu, nobles like the family of Ji exploited the common people, whose lives were harsh and difficult. Concerning this situation, Confucius, never protected the ruling class but kept on insisting that nobles be upright in their behavior. Once Ji Kangzi asked Confucius what was politics. Without hesitating, he answered, "politics is justice." If you set an example of being just, how will others not follow? Not long after that, Confucius declared more frankly that if one thought not about his own personal interest but rather stood upright and followed the straight path — people would obey him without his giving them orders to obey. If he did not behave right, and never kept his word, people would not follow him no matter how amiable his words sounded. In all these propositions, Confucius emphasized that rulers should set a good example. He dared to expose the simplest problem in social relationships, which at the same time was the hardest to follow for the ruling class. At the same time, Confucius warned the king that he was like a boat, while the common people were like water. Water could carry the boat, but also could turn it over. Common people could support the rule of the king as well as overthrow him. It was imperative to be wary of potential dangers during times of peace. The principle of benevolence and morality needs to be enforced to prevent social disturbances and prevent oneself from being overthrown.

Concerning the principle of governing with benevolence and morality, one of the important points was using qualified personnel. Those managing the country needed to be diligent and clean. Upright people needed to be used first of all, whose behavior could restrain and affect the greedy and incompetent officials. In this way, a country could be well managed. When his student Fan Chi asked him what was benevolence, he answered "loving people." When asked what was wisdom, he said "understanding people." Confucius connected the two and said, "If the position of the upright people could be raised above those of the evil ones, the evil people could become upright, too." When Zi Xia heard this from Fan Chi, he gasped in admiration, "How profound the meaning is!" When Shun was the emperor, he promoted Gao Tao. As a result, those without the quality of benevolence disappeared. When Tang was ruling the country, he chose Yiyin among many, with the same result.

Being a Senior Counselor of the State, Confucius many times told the king the importance of using qualified personnel. When the king asked him how to make people obey him, Confucius answered, "If you raise the position of the upright people above those of the evil ones, people will obey you. If not, people will never obey your order."

According to this principle, Confucius kept on urging his students to be successful at understanding people, using qualified people, promoting what was beneficial and abolishing what was harmful. Ran Yong once was the housekeeper for the family of Ji. Confucius told him to promote eminent people. As to how to recommend and promote talents, Confucius said, "Promote the ones you know and others will promote those you don't know." When Mi Zijian was the administrator at Shanfu (today's

Shan County in Shandong Province), he found out there were five wise men in the area. He invited them to his place and honored them as his teachers, asking them for suggestions on how to manage the place. Confucius praised him for doing something great. Because Mi Zijian put eminent people in important positions, the place was well managed. Confucius felt it was a pity that Shanfu was a place not big enough to have more influence. If this principle were to be used to manage a much bigger place, the benefit would be more influential.

In Confucius' opinion, people needed to follow rules and regulations in every aspect, including political matters, personal relationships, and daily life. If fish and meat had gotten rotten, he would not eat it. If meat were not cut in the way he considered proper, he would refuse to eat it. He wouldn't eat a dish if it were not cooked with enough spice. He would refuse to sit at the dinner table if it was not set properly. It was not proper to talk before going to sleep, nor was it proper to chat at a meal. One shouldn't have large meals when there was a funeral ceremony nearby. There were clear regulations concerning what to wear during each season and how to talk with different people. It showed that he wanted to obey every regulation in every single aspect. He had the habit of being careful with everything big or trivial, which was in accordance with his attitude on political matters.

In his personal life, Confucius was very cultured, following the principles of rites. In addition, he would never take money in a dishonest way. He would not be subservient to those sycophants in power just in order to get himself a high position in the imperial court. He said, "With roughage to eat, cold water to drink, and an arm to pillow the head, life can still be full of happiness. However, if I lived a rich life, but one that was gained through an improper way, that life to me would be the clouds floating in the sky." He was willing to live a simple life and considered it great enjoyment. Riches gotten improperly were like clouds, which would disappear at a glance — not worth admiring or pursuing.

A Society of Great Harmony

Confucius never ceased observing and studying society. At the same time, he used his views towards society to observe and study history. In his opinion, history kept on changing. Once when he stood on the bank of a river, seeing the river as it kept on flowing, he observed: "Time passes by just like this river, never stopping day or night."

His student Zi Zhang asked Confucius, "Is it possible to know what will happen after ten generations?"

"The Yin Dynasty inherited the culture of the Xia Dynasty with some changes," Confucius answered. "The same thing happened with the Zhou Dynasty after the Yin Dynasty. In this way, matters after a hundred generations — let alone 10 generations — can be approximately assumed." Although here Confucius only mentioned the inheritance of social institutions, he was noting the connection between things. He confirmed that history keeps on developing and changing. Again he said, "The culture of the Zhou Dynasty inherited that of the two dynasties preceding it and developed to be more

colorful and mature." Although this idea about change had some limitations, it had merits.

Based on this historical view, Confucius looked forward with optimism to the future. He many times mentioned this.

One day, he was sitting together with his students, Yan Hui and Zi Lu. He asked them to talk about their hopes and ambitions. Zi Lu said, "I would like to share my clothes, horses and carriages with my friends. I would not be angry if they were broken." Yan Hui said, "I would not brag if I did something good. Nor would I declare my successes before others."

These ideals were good, but not enough to satisfy Confucius. When asked to talk about his own, Confucius said, "The elderly would feel comfortable being with me. Friends would trust me. The young would remember me." If this could be done, it showed that he had contributed a lot to the society and people. Of course, Confucius had ambitions even bigger than these.

Once after the sacrificial ceremony in the 12th month according to the lunar calendar, Confucius talked about what he considered an ideal society:

If a society with great harmony were to be realized, that would be the time when this society would belong to all its members. People would choose eminent persons to manage the world. People would live in harmony and with loyalty to each other. Everybody would love not only his kinsman or his own children, but everyone else. The elderly would feel comfortable and safe in their remaining years. The middle-aged could focus on their work. The young would have someone to raise and educate them. The widowed, the lonely, and the disabled would all have some means to support them. Each man would have suitable work to do, while each woman would have somebody to lean on. Everything produced was owned by the public, not by any specific person. Everybody would feel it an honor to labor instead of being ashamed. They all would try their best in work. There would no longer be such things as cheating, seeking personal advantage, theft, or robbery. Since there would be no private property, there would be no need to shut the gate at night.

This was a picture of "the world as one community" and "a society of great harmony" that expressed the highest ideals of Confucius. It showed that Confucius advocated diligence in working, was against laziness and cheating, and was concerned about people's life and stability in the society — all these were reflected in his ideas about society. At that time, his ideas had positive implications.

With this ideal of a perfect world, Confucius realized that it would be difficult to accomplish this idea any time soon. He therefore further proposed the idea of a well-to-do society. That is, based on the situations of his time, it was necessary to strengthen the city wall and carry out the principle of rites and justice. When rites and justice were carried out, the ruler would behave properly according to his status, and so would the officials. Parents and children would love each other. Brothers would get along and couples would enjoy their relationship. Friends would be loyal to each other. Regulations would become complete, and production would be developed. The eminent and the fool could be distinguished. Common people could live a stable life. Compared with the perfect world of great harmony, this society was not good enough. However, it could help the country to be united and the society to be stable. At that time, this idea was a positive and progressive idea.

Talking About the Principles of Life While Observing the Instrument of Qi

Soon after he returned to the State of Lu, Confucius turned 70 which was considered a rather old age. Confucius described himself by saying: "I can do whatever I desire and not infringe rules and regulations." He thought at his age, he could see the nature of things with wisdom. When doing something he could stick to his own principles and at the same time enjoy much freedom. This is what he called the doctrine of the mean.

One day his student Zi Gong asked him, "Who is better, Zhuansun Shi or Bu Shang?" Confucius answered, "Zhuansun Shi tends to overdo it while Bu Shang is just the opposite." Zi Gong continued, "Then can I say Zhuansun Shi is better?" Confucius shook his head, "One is not better than the other. Neither of their ways is desirable."

This was Confucius' proposition — that excess was no better than deficiency. In the ancient books, there are stories of Confucius' talking about the principles while observing the instrument of Qi.

One day, Confucius led his students to visit the imperial temple. There they saw a container hung on a frame that looked like a container to hold wine, food, or water. It was not exactly vertical, but leaned to one side. Confucius felt curious enough to ask the temple caretaker about it. The caretaker told him that this instrument was called Qi, hung at the right side of the temple as a warning to people. Immediately Confucius remembered.

"I ever heard that there was an instrument named Qi placed at the right side of the seat in the temple. It leans to one side when empty. When you add water, it will turn upside down if filled, but will stay right side up if half filled." The caretaker nodded his head. Getting his permission, Confucius ordered his students to fill the container with water. One student filled it full, and it immediately turned upside down. When every drop of water was poured out, it returned to its former position. Another student slowly added water into it. When it was half filled, it stood vertical.

The students were deeply absorbed by this scene. Confucius, however, gave a long sigh and said with much significance, "Everything under heaven will overturn if it is too full. There is no exception."

Then Zi Lu asked, "Is it possible to be rich forever, and never to have any frustration or failure?" With the help of this instrument, Confucius understood the doctrine of the mean and answered by developing this doctrine further.

"Certainly it is possible — but only if one is wise enough not to show it, but pretends to be stupid. You need to be humble even if you are successful and all people under heaven receive benefits from what you have done. You need to be patient and careful — as if you had no ability at all — even if nobody can compete with your bravery and courage. You need to be economical and clean even if you are rich enough to own the whole world. Those who can control themselves are wise. One can avoid frustration and failure if he is wise."

This expressed the philosophy of Confucius' golden mean, which includes the ideas that people with wisdom should appear to be stupid; those with strength should not be proud; those with courage should not be cruel; those with wealth should be thrifty. Using this method to get along in this world, one will not meet failure at any time.

Confucius told his students, "If wrong ideas were criticized, misfortunes could be prevented." He claimed people "could be different and at the same time united." The precondition should be unity. If people agreed with each other on major issues, they had the possibility to cooperate. If not, there was no way to be in accord or to sacrifice one for the other. The relationship between things was mutual. If the relationship was well handled, people could supplement each other and develop together by helping each other. If not, they would have conflicts with each other to diminish each other's strength. Confucius meant the same thing when he said, "People with different views cannot look for cooperation."

Confucius never stopped emphasizing flexibility in dealing with things. "There is no definite answer to the question as yes or no," he said. He praised a senior official in the State of Wei named Qu Boyu, who came out to be an official when the political state was liberal but hid his ability when it was tyrannical. He commented that it was a shame for one not to seek a position in the government when the political situation was good enough. However, it still would be a shame if one sought to be an official when the political state was not in a good condition. The same matter, under different situations, should be treated with different perspectives and handled with different methods.

Concerning the cultivation of one's morality, Confucius said the poor should not be troubled all day by poverty. Instead, they should seek happiness in life. The rich should not act wildly against law and public opinion. The more riches one has, the more strictly he should follow the principles of good behavior. A gentleman should be solemn and serious, avoiding fighting others over petty issues. He should get along well with others, but at the same time should avoid forming cliques. Concerning study, Confucius thought that studying and thinking should be combined. Without thinking, study could not be profound and deep. So, it was useless to study in this way. What you had learned could not be used. Without studying for new knowledge, your idea soon would be exhausted. Others described his appearance: "Confucius is strict as well as being mild. He is dignified, but not severe. He is humble and peaceful at the same time."

As for drinking, Confucius said, "There is no limitation on drinking. It is better not to over drink." Everything had a standard, including drinking. Some people could drink more than others. Although there was a variety and difference concerning this matter, nobody should become drunk, exceeding his limitation. From these words it could be seen that everything was connected with those which were in conflict with or different than others. This was expressed as a "degree" or "limit." Everything should be done according to a certain degree, not surpassing its limits. Going to extremes should be avoided. All these showed Confucius inherited the ancient Emperor Yao's idea: "It is better to hold the middle," and "It is better to choose the middle position for everything that needs to be done."

In regard to society, this idea of the mean or in the middle was expressed in rites. Confucius regarded rites as the principle behind relationship between people that could distinguish as well as connect people belonging to different hierarchical positions. For both parties, rites helped them to control themselves and bring accord to their relationship. Therefore, Confucius thought rites could help to control and govern people. At the same time, rites could help the rulers and the ruled get along well with each other. In this way, both could work to stabilize the society. This showed his idea:

"When rites are carried out, harmony is the most important issue. How beautiful the principles of the ancient kings are."

"Harmony is most important" between people with different social positions, Confucius said. This principle proved to be quite effective in the days of ancient times, and so it should be today. Therefore, after he said this to his student You Ruo, Confucius continued, "It would not do if people try to create harmony for the sake of being harmonious without the regulation of rites."

Confucius regarded the doctrine of the mean as the highest of all. He regretted that the morality of people was degraded and that nobody at that time followed the doctrine of the mean.

"The doctrine of the mean is a virtue. It is very rare today that somebody can follow this principle," Confucius said.

The doctrine of the mean was the highest standard for a man to follow. Among his students, Yan Hui was the one who had mastered this principle and could put it into practice. Yan Hui could "deal with everything appropriately. Whenever he learned something useful, he would immediately write it down."

Confucius' idea of the doctrine of the mean stayed with him all his life. This principle has had a long history. The ancient Emperor of Yao taught his successor that "it would be better to hold to the middle." As a result, a time of prosperity developed under the reign of Emperor Yao and Emperor Shun, his successor, when "every state under heaven was united." King Wen of the Zhou Dynasty developed the Eight Diagrams created by Fuxi into *The Book of Changes*. In this book, the idea of dialectic and the doctrine of the mean appear many times. When Confucius studied this book, the thread, which was made of cattle skin to hold the bamboo slips together, broke several times. In his late years, he still desired to learn more from this book to avoid major mistakes in life. When he studied this book, he kept notes of what he had read. These were known as "the ten wings," that formed the base for Confucius' philosophical ideas.

Teaching at Xingtan
(Apricot Forum)

Having begun teaching at the age of 30, Confucius never ceased training students all his life. He emphasized educating the common people during his political career, and he took advantage of opportunities to use various means to train and teach his students. During the six or seven years following his return to the State of Lu until his death, Confucius devoted his time and energy mainly to teaching. During his many years of teaching, he kept on practicing and developing new teaching methods. His achievements covered many aspects, from content to method, from theory to practice — contributing much to China's history, even the world's history, of education.

Confucius determined that people's "nature is similar, but their habits are different." Therefore, Confucius thought that education could change a person's character and personality. He claimed that all people were subject to change, including himself. He described the development of his thoughts vividly as the following:

"When I was 15, I set my mind on learning. At 30, I became well-established in my career; at 40, I was no longer influenced by others; at 50, I knew the fate determined by heaven; at 60, I understood the true meaning behind the words of others; at 70, even following the desires of my heart, I would not exceed the rules."

Confucius' dividing his whole life into several stages described a regular pattern in the development of one's thinking. So it is necessary to receive continuous education to assure development in the right direction.

Confucius' aim in teaching was very clear: To train qualified people who could manage the country. His student Zi Xia always said: "An official must learn in order to be qualified, while one who is good at learning must become an official."

This is a fine reflection of the aim of Confucius in education: One who is managing the state needs to keep on learning so as to be qualified in better serving his own class or community. The purpose of his teaching students was to select the competent ones and send them to be officials so that what they learned could be used in assisting the governance of the country. Therefore, the focus of his teaching was moral education, in other words, education about ideology. The emphasis was on rites and music — the important events happening in the society and country.

Rites, in Confucius' mind, included those regulations and policies formulated in the early years of the Western Zhou Dynasty, and other standards governing the behavior of various classes. All these were important means to ensure the existence of the slavery system. One of his students, Lin Fang, once asked him what was the nature of rites. And Confucius answered that it was the greatest and most fundamental matter under heaven. Once in his yard, when he saw his son, Kong Li walking by, he asked, "Have you learned rites?" The young man answered, "Not yet." Confucius immediately said, "If one doesn't study rites, there is no way for him to be a man in the world." Therefore, it can be seen that Confucius put much emphasis on rites.

Music, being a means to accompany education on rites, was always mentioned together with rites. Confucius also put much attention on music as he did on rites. When he was in the State of Qi, he made a trip to listen to the music by Emperor Shun, the successor, and praised that music as excellent. According to his standard, music needed not only to have good form, but also had to carry the meaning of peace, goodness, and elegance. He was against the lascivious music of the Zheng State, thinking that this music would distort the elegance in music just as immoral people would violate the rules of a country. He himself could play Qin (a string instrument) and Qing (a percussion instru ment), as well as express himself through singing. He employed the forms of rites and music to carry out ideological education, which was an important aspect of his education process.

An important part of political education was moral and personal development. He advocated morality cultivation and self-examination, and asked people "to imitate those who are righteous, but to examine oneself when seeing those who are not righteous." Seeing good people should inspire one to learn from them; seeing those who are bad should lead to self-examination to see if anything similar in one's self needs to be changed. His student Zeng Shen once said, "I examine myself three times a day," which showed that Confucius kept on emphasizing this point on his students.

Confucius believed that people should have spirit. "In the coldest days, you can see pine trees remain green while other plants wither," he said. And: "An army can survive without a commander, but not if common soldiers lose their spirit." An army can go on fighting without any commander only if every soldier will stick with it. However, for anybody, nothing can be achieved if spirit is lost. While requiring others to be humble, respectful, and careful, he himself behaved the same way, being amiable and respectable. He asked his students to be good at making friends, picking out those who were worth making friends with and to master courtesy and manners. To sum up, Confucius thought that a man needed to be a gentleman and mature person through study and training to ultimately become a virtuous man.

Education practiced before Confucius emphasized the teaching of politics and history. In response to the requirements of social development, Confucius added more issues to his teaching. He taught his students "six skills," namely, rites, music, archery, riding, writing, and arithmetic. Rites included important state affairs, regulations and rules, laws and proverbs, activities of the nobles and means of governing. Music, through creating a certain desired atmosphere, incorporated the teaching of rites. Archery referred to various military and athletic activities. Riding referred to the driving of carts, including chariots during battles and various kinds of other carts on which nobles would often ride. It also referred to those who drove a cart through the states publicizing their propositions and engaged in diplomatic or political activities. Writing also included one's mastery of and taste for literature, as well as observation and study of history and society. Besides simple calculation, arithmetic also included other skills and knowledge about nature.

Through the study of the "six skills," the students of Confucius were equipped with various abilities. In his teaching, he emphasized: "Documents, practice, loyalty, and faithfulness." Besides the study of documents, history, and philosophy — students should practice what they had learned, and should have loyalty and faithfulness when dealing with others. All these meant thorough teaching and training. Considering the different characteristics of his students, Confucius emphasized different aspects for different students. "Four subjects" were included: Morality, oration, executive management and literature. Under the subject of morality, Confucius mainly trained students with good morality who might be qualified to manage the country. They included Yan Yuan, Min Ziqian, Ran Boniu, Ran Zhonggong, etc. In oration, he mainly trained those who were good at giving speeches and debating, skillful at diplomatic affairs, such as Zai Yu and Zi Gong. In executive management, he mainly trained students who had talent for managing administrative affairs under dukes, princes and high officials. They included Ran Qiu and Zhong You, who worked as housekeepers for the family of Ji. In literature, Confucius trained those with a high taste for literature who could write articles expressing the ideas of the Confucian school, for example, Zi You and Zi Xia.

When teaching, Confucius followed actual teaching materials. In his later years, he collated some literature and documents from ancient times. Actually he was editing these materials for teaching purpose. After revising and abridging *The Book of Songs*, he used it as the text for literary study to improve the level of literary appreciation and expression of his students. Confucius employed *Collection of Ancient Texts*, which recorded history of the previous generations, as a way for students to learn history by absorbing the experiences of the ancestors in political activities. His students studied various ceremonial regulations formulated in the early Zhou Dynasty and mastered skills of playing various musical instruments in such ceremonies. They studied the philosophical ideas in *The Book of Changes* so that these ideas could be used in observing society and life. *The Spring and Autumn Annals* were composed based on the history of the Lu State. Through studying history of recent times, students could have a clear view about contemporary political situation in the country and then establish their own views on political events. From these materials it can be seen that Confucius encouraged his students to know as much as possible and to master as many skills as possible so that they could become people with various abilities. In what he taught, some of his ideas were also expressed, that is, the king should be respected and obeyed, and "individuals can promote established doctrines."

During the time of Confucius, there was not such a thing as teaching a class. Therefore, there were no definite places of teaching. Sometimes Confucius had fixed places to teach while other times not. During the stable times such as before being involved in political activities and after returning to the State of Lu, he taught students near Queli, where he lived. During those days when he was occupied with political activities, especially when travelling through states, he taught his students whenever and wherever possible. In the chapter of "Fisherman" in *The Book of Zhuang Zi*, it was recorded that "Confucius traveled in the area of Ziwei and lectured sitting on the altar of Xingtan." Later records all said that Confucius taught students in Xingtan. Even though the exact place cannot be traced, it must be a place near the city of Lu. Teaching at the altar of Xingtan became a symbol of the teaching career of Confucius. Later people built a Xingtan in the temple of Confucius in Qufu.

When Confucius taught students, he adopted many methods. It was not just a teacher who was speaking and students who were listening. Sometimes students would ask questions and Confucius would answer them. Sometimes Confucius would ask his students some questions and ask them to make comments. Sometimes students would have group discussions, and Confucius would give a summary. Sometimes he would comment on people of previous and contemporary times while revealing his own thoughts at the same time. At other times he would let one or several students express their own thoughts and opinions. Sometimes it was group work

while other times it might be specific training. Sometimes the place was fixed while others not. Sometimes he would give a positive answer and sometimes a negative one. Sometimes what he said amounted to a summary, and sometimes an analysis. Sometimes it was a description, other times it might be a recollection. Sometimes he would make a comment while other times an argument.

Confucius was very honest. He told students not to pretend that they knew something when they did not. He was against those who pretended to know, especially those who acted as if they knew everything. In his opinion, one should first of all listen and look, and then choose what was good and beneficial. He also argued that theory and knowledge should be meditated on after being learned and then should be put into practice. Under his comprehensive teaching, more than 3,000 students were trained, of whom more than 70 mastered all the six skills. At that time, a Confucian school, with a large number of followers, came into being as a result. Confucius, being a great educator, was honored as the model of teachers for generations to come.

True Respect Between Teacher and Students

Confucius was an educational theorist as well as an experienced teacher. His career in education lasted some 50 years, calculated from the time he was over twenty years old until his death. Especially during those days after his returning to the State of Lu, the close relationship between Confucius and his students was especially evident.

Being a teacher, Confucius himself was always ready to learn from others. In his opinion, only with noble character and extensive knowledge could one be a teacher. He himself pursued moral excellence, carried out charity activities, loved people, treasured talented people, was actively involved in state affairs, and remained loyal to kings. He set a good example for his students in every aspect. For example, when talking about learning from others, he said, "If there are three men walking together, one of them is bound to be good enough to be my teacher."

He believed that one should be modest in learning and should never be ashamed of learning from those who appeared to be inferior. When others praised him, he remained sober and merely said, "I was not born with this knowledge. I only love history and am quick to learn what I want to know." He never considered himself a born genius, but emphasized that his knowledge had been gained through his efforts. Once he told his student Zi Gong, "If you want to finish a task, you need to sharpen your tools first of all." In his opinion, a good craftsman must first of all have good tools to do a job well. Similarly, if a man wants to be good at work he must have knowledge. He himself followed this principle, and his students all followed his example.

Being a good teacher, Confucius loved his work and tried to find better teaching methods to do the job well. He always said that he was never tired of teaching. He said to his students, "Do you think I hide something from you? No, I have nothing to hide. I am completely open and honest towards you. That's just me." He was honest to students. Naturally, the students would respect him.

Confucius was good at applying different teaching methods to different students. Among his students he could see that Gao Chai was slow, Zeng Shen was simple, Zhuansun Shi liked to go to extremes, Zhong You was imprudent, Ran Qiu was timid, and Bu Shang was not mature enough in his behavior. When several students stood next to him, he could see clearly their different character. Min

Ziqian would look respectful and upright beside Confucius, while Ran You and Zi Gong would appear soft and happy.

Based on his thorough understanding of his students, Confucius taught them in different ways. One day, Zi Lu asked Confucius, "If I start to do it immediately after I hear about a matter, is that OK?" Confucius answered, "If your father and brother are with you, it is better to consult them first. How could you start doing something only at hearing about it?"

When Ran Qiu asked him the same question, Confucius immediately said, "Do it if you want to." Gongxi Hua, another student, felt quite puzzled at his giving different answers to the same question. Confucius explained to him, "Ran Qiu usually is very hesitant in acting, therefore, I encourage him to take action immediately. While for Zi Lu, he is brave and seldom considers much before acting, therefore, I would like to restrain him a little bit."

Confucius based his teaching on understanding students and was against those who followed rigid rules in teaching and spoon-fed their students, never inspiring them to think independently. Confucius said: "Those who keep on learning without thinking will get confused, while those who never stop thinking without taking in new knowledge will get tired." If you only focus on books and never takes some time to think, you will gradually get confused and lost. On the contrary, if you never stop thinking, never seriously read books or absorb experiences of others, soon you will get exhausted. Only when you think carefully before you start to do something, would it be possible to do it well. He advised his students not to depend solely on assumptions, not to be too certain, not to be stubborn, nor self-centered whenever they did something. Confucius always said to his students, "Once I depleted my brain by thinking without meals or sleep; however, nothing beneficial turned out. Only after I turned to books, did my thinking become rich."

Confucius taught his students that those who know the necessity of study are not as good as those who like to study, while those who like to study are not as good as those who regarded study as their pleasure. If one regards study as an enjoyment, efficiency will be much improved and increased. Confucius, first of all, encouraged his students' own initiative. Then he would teach them and guide their improvement. In his teaching he always encouraged and inspired his students. He said, "If one doesn't have a strong will, one will achieve nothing. If a person doesn't have the desire to learn but you teach that person how to do it, that person won't be inspired to learn. If you teach a person one thing, but that person doesn't know how to follow through to learn more, this student is not worth teaching. Teach that person no more." Confucius thought that only when the student had a strong desire to know something, should a teacher begin to teach him. If you told him where the east was, but he still did not know where the other three directions were, then teach him no more. Through his inspiration, his students could use their brains to think about how it was instead of only knowing what it was. They knew how to infer from one matter to the others, thus, "knowing one meant knowing ten."

Confucius put much emphasis on reviewing so that his students could master what they had learned. The first chapter of *The Analects* says, "Isn't it a pleasure to review what you have learned?" In his opinion, it was very interesting to review and restudy what one had learned before. He also said, "If somebody knows to review what he has learned and to study what he needs to know, he will be competent to be a teacher." In his opinion, only after one had mastered what he knew, could he have new understanding and make further improvement.

Confucius also told his students that it was important to practice what they had learned. He maintained that one should be "slow in talking and quick in acting." It was far better to take action than to talk a lot of empty words. If you wanted to know somebody, it was better to watch his behavior than listen to his words. As for practicing, he thought people of his generation were not as good as those before them. People of previous generations were afraid of breaking promises, while contemporary people often broke their promises. Confucius emphasized that what one had learned was for use, especially principles for managing the country and governing the people. Many students had successful experiences in this aspect.

It was obvious that Confucius loved and protected his students. He thought the younger generation would surpass the older. He once praised his student Zi Gong as someone who had the manner to conduct himself on formal occasions, and told another student, Ran Yong, that he would have a promising future. Min Ziqian claimed that there was no need to build another storehouse in the State of Lu, which Confucius confirmed. He immediately criticized Zai Yu for disobeying him. Many times he praised Yan Hui, who was diligent in studying, and asked others to follow his example. Once Zi Lu showed conceitedness while playing the Qin. Confucius criticized him, saying that Zi Lu had not learned how to play Qin from him. This criticism was so severe that some fellow students began to show disrespect towards Zi Lu. After hearing of it, Confucius corrected the mistake he had made and said, "When Zi Lu is playing Qin, he is like a man who enters the hall but hasn't yet entered the inner rooms." This meant Zi Lu's skill in playing Qin was not bad, but at the same time not good enough. This comment was more suitable. He paid a personal visit to Ran Boniu when Ran was ill. When Yan Hui passed away, he was very sad. It could be seen that Confucius had a very close relationship with his students.

Confucius loved his students, so naturally he was respected by them. Zi Lu, a bold man at the beginning, didn't treat Confucius with due respect. But Confucius never ceased loving and educating him. Zi Lu went with him wherever he went. Once Confucius said that if nobody offered him a government position or if he wandered to the sea, Zi Lu would go with him. Zi Gong said that their teacher was so knowledgeable that nobody could compare with him but the sun and moon in the sky. The knowledge of Confucius was as high as the sky, and no ladder could reach it.

It was recorded in ancient books that after Confucius passed away, his students missed him so much that they had no desire to eat or sleep. Later they got an idea. They asked a fellow student, You Ruo, who looked very much like their teacher, to get dressed in Confucius' clothes and sit every day in his seat. Certainly they felt quite comforted. Not long afterwards, Zeng Shen said that the teacher was as deep as the big rivers and as warm as the sun in autumn. Nobody could be compared with him. Then they gave up this dressing-up idea. Having the idea showed their longing for their teacher, while giving up the idea showed their respect for him.

According to rules of the Zhou Dynasty, when parents and teachers passed away, children and students should mourn for three years. When Confucius passed away, all his students mourned him for three years beside his tomb. Zi Gong was especially close with his teacher. He built a cottage next to the tomb, and went on mourning for another three years. Even today, you can see Zi Gong's Mourning Cottage next to Confucius' tomb in Quhua of Shangdong Province. This cottage stands to represent this story, which shows how much respect a student could have for his teacher.

The Three Thousand Elite Students

In a lifetime of teaching, Confucius trained many outstanding students. Some people have said that the number of his students reached 3,000. This, of course, is an estimation, but one that suggests to us that the number of his students was large. Among the 3,000, more than 70 are said to have mastered all the six skills. Thirty-two are mentioned in *The Analects*. *The Record of History* offers biographies on 77 of Confucius' students. In the *Analects of the Confucian Family*, *Important History of the Tang Dynasty*, and *Documents of Queli*, 72 are mentioned as outstanding students of Confucius. In 739 AD in the 27th year under the reign of Xuanzong Emperor in the Tang Dynasty, sacrifices were offered to 77 students. In the early years of the Song Dynasty (960-1279), the number was 72, and in the late years of the Northern Song Dynasty under the reign of Daguan (1107-1110), the number increased to 82. Under the reign of Gaozong Emperor in the Southern Song Dynasty, it was said that 72 was the right number, while under the reign of Emperor

Jiajing (1522-1566), the number was 76. Later in the early years of the Qing Dynasty (1644-1911), more were added to make the number 80. Among these students, some learned directly from Confucius, while others indirectly. Some admired Confucius so much that they called themselves students of him. Some others might have been mentioned by chance in some books, or might have gotten in touch with him and were overwhelmed by his morality and knowledge. All these were included as students of Confucius. According to statistics, all together 98 names can be traced through records. The following is a brief introduction to some of the major ones.

Yan Hui, also called Yan Yuan, was a native of the State of Lu, and 30 years junior to Confucius. He was born into a humble family. Confucius said that Yan Hui "lived on one meal and cold water every day in a humble lane." Though his situation was hard, he was diligent at learning and was very clever, understanding ten matters after hearing about one of them. Being one of Confucius' favorite students, he was listed by his teacher as the top student under the subject of morality. His moral character was so noble that he could well control himself and carry out principles of rites. It was rare for Confucius to describe anybody with the word of benevolence, but he once said that Yan Hui "hadn't done anything to violate the principle of benevolence for three months." Yan Hui had strong self-discipline and found contentment in poverty. Even though without any desire to be an official, he had the hope to manage a country and make it into a peaceful and prosperous society. Confucius praised him often because whenever Confucius talked with students, Yan Hui's answer would excel those of others.

Min Sun, with the literal name of Ziqian, was a native of the State of Lu, and 15 years junior to Confucius. He, too, was a student under the subject of morality. He was quiet but filial to his parents. When he was young he lost his mother, and his stepmother treated him badly. When his father found out about it, he wanted to send her back to her parents' home. Min Sun begged his father to let the stepmother stay. As a consequence, the whole family stayed together, living a happy life. Another story has it that the state wanted to build another treasury, which was unnecessary, and Min Sun opposed the idea to save people's labor. This gained Confucius' confirmation.

Ran Geng, with the literal name of Bo Niu, was a native of the State of Lu and 16 years junior to Confucius. He was highly praised during the Warring States Period because he, together with Min Sun and Yan Hui, was considered to represent Confucius in every aspect while the respected students of Confucius like Zi Xia, Zi You, and Zi Zhang were believed to have inherited from Confucius only a certain aspect of his thinking. Unfortunately Ran Geng was struck by a fatal disease. Confucius went to his house to visit him and felt very sorry to lose this student when he died.

Ran Yong, with the literal name of Zhong Gong, was the half-brother of Ran Geng and 20 years junior to Confucius. He was born into a humble family. However, Confucius said in praise of him, "Though born like a calf by a farm ox, he had the skin and horn of a noble heritage." Confucius saw a promising future for Ran Yong even though this student lacked oratory skills to go along with his quality of benevolence. Confucius was not worried about his lacking of oratory skill and comforted him, "If you have benevolence, what is the necessity of talking a lot about empty things?" Later when Ran Yong became the housekeeper for the family of Ji, he consulted Confucius about how things should be done. His teacher told him to be diligent in working, to be quick in forgiving others, and to be ready to recommend qualified people.

Ran Qiu, also called Ran You, with the literal name of Zi You, was the younger brother of Ran Yong and 28 years junior to Confucius. He was talented in management and was listed as the first one under the subject of executive management. Confucius said Ran Qiu was versatile. He followed Confucius in his travels among the states but returned one year earlier than his teacher to the State of Lu. Being invited to work for the family of Ji, he helped his master to defeat the State of Qi in the second year after he began to work for Master Ji. He was placed in a very important position, and as a result, Master Ji invited Confucius to return to the state.

Zhong You, with the literal name of Zi Lu, was a native of Bianyi (today's Sishui in Shandong Province) in the State of Lu and nine years younger than Confucius. Although born into a humble family, Zi Lu had a talent in management. When Confucius was an official in the State of Lu, Zi Lu was the steward of Master Ji. When Confucius stayed in the State of Wei, Zi Lu was the housekeeper in the county of Pu. After Confucius returned to the State of Lu, Zi Lu first worked for Master Ji then went to work as the governor in Kongli. Later he died in a civil war in the State of Wei. Actively supporting and carrying out Confucius' idea of governing the country according to established rites, Zi Lu was never afraid of difficulties. Being impetuous, he sometimes would act heedlessly. He often came to Confucius with strange questions, and the teacher either gave him answers or criticized him. Confucius especially appreciated Zi Lu's character of frankness and self-criticism. Their relationship was honest and sincere.

Duanmu Ci, with the literal name of Zi Gong, was a native of the State of Wei and 31 years junior to Confucius. He was the most talented student in the subject of diplomacy. He accompanied with success the Duke and officials of the State of Lu in their diplomatic activities. Being also good at business, he conducted some business as he followed and learned from Confucius. Later he got very rich. He was quick and could soon understand what his teacher was thinking about. He respected and admired his teacher, while at the same time he was able to understand and comfort Confucius. After the death of Confucius, he went on mourning for six years, three years longer than others. This demonstrates how much he respected and missed his teacher.

Zai Yu, with the literal name of Zi Wo, was from the State of Lu and was 29 years younger than Confucius. He was good at speech. Being an active thinker, he often asked Confucius some unexpected questions. Once he doubted the regulation that children should go on mourning for three years after their parents passed away. He even questioned Confucius about the possibility of carrying out the principle of benevolence. When Confucius toured among the states, Zai Yu was sent to the State of Chu as a representative. Some books recorded that he was once the Dafu of Linzi in the State of Qi.

Yan Yan, with the literal name of Zi You, was a native of the State of Wu in the south and was 45 years junior to Confucius. He was known for his mastery of literary books and historical documents. He — with Zi Xia and Zi Zhang — is listed as one of the three young students in the late years of Confucius. He had many ideals and paid much attention to rites and music. When he was the governor in the City of Wu in the State of Lu, Yan Yan managed the city according to the principle of rites and music, which was praised by his teacher.

Bu Shang, with the literal name of Zi Xia, was from the State of Wei and was 44 years younger than his teacher. He was born into a poor and humble family, and he himself was very slim and weak when he was young. After he began to follow Confucius, gradually he became very good at certain aspects. Being quick in learning and active in thinking, he was regarded as one of the most eminent students in the late years of Confucius. He once worked as the governor of Jufu. He helped his teacher with the collecting and collating of ancient documents and literary works. Confucius said that Bu Shang gave him much inspiration in the study of poetry because the latter would always come up with some unique opinions concerning *The Book of Songs*. After Confucius passed away, he went to lecture in the State of Wei, being the teacher of the Duke. Many outstanding scholars in the Warring States Period were his students.

Zhuansun Shi, with the literal name of Zi Zhang, was from the State of Chen and was 48 years younger than Confucius. A handsome young man, he was born into a humble family. He was once a middleman in the trade of horses. After learning from Confucius, he became quite knowledgeable and in his late years also taught students in the State of Chen, and his influence was widespread. He had great ambitions, but sometimes paid too much attention to the appearance rather than the true nature of things. However, he tried to follow the principle of benevolence in his behavior, and being tolerant, was willing to accept different types of people.

Zeng Shen, with the literal name of Zi Yu, was a native of the State of Lu, and was 46 years younger than Confucius. He was born into a family of poor farmers, with his father Zeng Dian also a student of Confucius. He was an easy-going and careful man. Confucius gave him *The Book of Fidelity* for his being quite filial to his parents. Being a faithful student of Confucius, he strictly followed his teacher's instruction in two aspects: benevolence and self-examination. He was very strict with himself, and was especially concerned with loyalty and fidelity. He thought Confucius' teaching could be expressed in two words: loyalty and forgiveness. He was a key link in the dissemination of Confucianism: He passed the teaching of Confucius to Kong Ji, the grandson of Confucius, who in turn passed it to Mencius, the second representative of Confucianism.

Besides the most famous 12 students mentioned above, others include:

Tantai Mieming, a native of the State of Lu, was atrocious in appearance but lofty in nature.

Mi Buqi, with the literal name of Zi Jian, was a native of the State of Lu and the governor of Shanfu for some time.

Yuan Xian, with the literal name of Zi En, was a native of the State of Lu and content with humble life.

Gongye Chang, a native of the State of Lu and Confucius' son-in-law, was once put into prison although innocent of any wrongdoing and was known for his good character.

Nangong Shi, also called Nan Rong, advocated morality and was the husband of Confucius' niece.

Gong Xi'ai, also called Ji Ci, was a native of the State of Qi. He was a person of moral integrity who refused to serve in the government.

Zeng Dian, also called Zeng Xi, had great ambitions and was Zeng Shen's father.

Yan Wuyao, with the literal name of Lu, was Yan Hui's father and a student of Confucius in his early teachings.

Shang Qu, with the literal name of Zi Mu, taught *The Book of Changes* to later generations.

Gao Chai, with the literal name of Zi Gao, was a talented native of the State of Wei, small in stature, however.

Qidiao Kai, with the literal name of Zi Kai, or Zi Ruo, was diligent in learning, brave and good at fighting battles, but never sought to be an official.

Sima Geng, with the literal name of Zi Niu, was a native of the State of Song.

Fan Xu, also called Fan Chi, was brave and good at fighting.

You Ruo, with the literal name of Zi You, was similar to Confucius in appearance and good at memorizing and thinking.

Gong Xichi, with the literal name of Zi Hua, knew well the rules and regulations in the wedding and funeral ceremonies.

Some other students were included in the *Book of History*, such as Gong Boliao, Liang Zhan, Yan Xing, Ran Ru, Cao Xu, Bo Qian, Gongsun Long, Ran Ji, Gongzu Juci, Qin Zu, Qidiao Duo, Qidiao Tufu, Lang Sichi, Shang Ze, Shi Zuoshu, Ren Buqi, Gong Liangru, Hou Chu, Qin Ran, Gong Xiayu, Xi Rongdian, Gongjian Ding, Yan Zu, Qiao Dan, Gou Jingjiang, Han Fuhei, Qin Shang, Shen Dang, Yan Zhipu, Rong Qi, Xuan Cheng, Zuo Renying, Yan Ji, Zheng Guo, Qin Fei, Shi Zhichang, Yan Kuai, Bu Shucheng, Yuan Kangji, Yue Kai, Lian Jie, Shu Zhonghui, Yan He, Di Hei, Bang Xun, Kong Zhong, Gongxi Yuru, Gongxi Dian and Xuan Dan.

Some others who were also found in such books as *The Analects, Mencius, The Book of Rites, Zuo Zhuan, Zhuang Zi, Yanzi's Spring and Autumn Annals* and *The*

Family Quotations of Confucius are: Lin Fang, Qin Lao, Chen Kang, Shen Chen, Qu Yuan, Gongsun Qiao, Ru Bei, Yan Gao, Mu Pi, Gongwang Zhiqiu, Xu Dian, Zhongsun Heji, Zhong Sunyue, Chang Ji, Ju Yu, Kong Xuan, Hui Shulan, Yan Zhuozou, Lian Jie, Zi Fuhe, and Zuoqiu Ming.

Collecting and Editing Ancient Books

During the seven years following his return to Lu, Confucius dedicated himself to editing ancient books. As a nation with a long history, China had many ancient books kept by government officially and unofficially by the late years of the Spring and Autumn Period. But many books were destroyed in wars; some were in the hands of upper class officials; and some were among the common people, remaining uncollected. Confucius made great contributions by collecting *The Book of Songs*, revising the rites and music, editing *The Book of Changes* and writing *The Spring and Autumn Annals*.

In the early years of Western Zhou, the king of Zhou regulated rites and composed music, establishing the systems in politics, economy and culture. But in the late years of the Spring and Autumn Period, rites and systems were destroyed, and the society of the time was in a great disorder. When Confucius was young, considering that the ancient books were incomplete and full of mistakes, Confucius was determined to collect ancient books and

develop traditional culture. In his late years when it was impossible for him to do anything in politics, Confucius thought it was the best time to do something for traditional culture. During the six or seven years between the time of his return to Lu and the time of his death, Confucius collected *The Book of Songs*, *Collection of Ancient Texts*, *The Book of Rites*, *The Book of Music*, *The Book of Changes* and *The Spring and Autumn Annals*, which are called by later generations "The Six Classics."

In the late years of the Spring and Autumn Period, with fluctuations in the economy and turmoil in politics, many poetic and musical works were lost. Many adept professional musicians for the rites fled to other areas: Zhi, the senior master of Lu, fled to the state of Qi; Gan, the musician of Lu, to Chu; Liao to Cai; and Que to Qin. Fang Shu, a drum player, fled to live by the Yellow River; Wu, a small drum player fled to live by the Han River; and Yang, a junior master, and Xiang, a chime stone player, went to live by the seaside. As a music lover and an earnest defender of slave system with rites and music, Confucius could do nothing but try to think hard on how to help his state out of this crisis. When Confucius was young, he had learned musical theory from Chang Hong and learned to play Qin, a seven-stringed plucked instrument in some ways similar to the zither, from Shi Xiang. As soon as he arrived at Qi, he went to listen to the music of Shao.

When he discussed music with the senior musician of Lu, he said that the standard music should be like this: When the music is played, it starts with a strict union and then more liberty; but the tone always remains clear, harmonious, brilliant, consistent, right until the end. This shows that he has a great accomplishment in music.

In Confucius' eyes, music was something concerned with politics. He thought that the music of a flourishing state should be peaceful and tranquil while the music of a disorderly state sounded furious and complaining; the music of a state before its destruction sounds sad. Therefore, we can determine that the state must have been suffering from calamity. To examine politics through rites and music, Confucius collected many music works and made comments on them. In his late years, this task had almost been completed. Confucius once said: "The music was not right until I returned to Lu from the State of Wei. 'Odes,' 'Hymn' and other music pieces are now all catalogued and revised " But unfortunately, *The Book of Music*, which is said to have been collected by Confucius, has been lost.

Poetry, the lines composed to accompany music in ancient times, is closely related to music, and it is said that some traces of *The Book of Music* can still be seen in *The Book of Rites*.

The Book of Songs, the earliest anthology of poems of China, which was written approximately in the 500 years between the Western Zhou and Spring and Autumn Period, vividly portrays through artistic imagery the social life and living conditions of the people of the time. It is said that *The Book of Songs* once had more than 3000 poems, but after Confucius' collecting and editing it was reduced to 305 poems. The authors of the original poems included both the nobles and common people living within the vast land between the reaches of the Yellow River and the Han River. Originally diversified in language and style, most of the poems in *The Book of Songs* now are poems of four-character lines, with the same rhymes. The structures and the repetitive rhyming system are nearly the same, which shows that all these poetry had been edited. And it is Confucius who is said to have edited them. *The Book of Songs* is composed of three sections, namely "Songs," "Odes," and "Hymns." Due to his efforts in collecting these poems, Confucius was familiar with them so much that he could sing them accompanied by the zither.

The collection and spread of *The Book of Songs* contributed greatly to the development of China's culture and art. It is an epoch-making book in the history of China's classical literature. The social system, customs and relations among people of the time are so vividly portrayed and represented through the poetry that the book has become a valuable reference source for historical researchers.

In ancient China, some officials were appointed to be responsible for recording history. Speeches were recorded by the official called zuoshi while events were recorded by youshi. *Collection of Ancient Texts* is a document of politics and history in the style of remark-keeping (i.e. prayers, instructions, oaths, admonitions). Some remarks were the records of the time, and some were taken down by later generation according to their recollections. In view of the chronological order, *Collection of Ancient Texts* is divided into *The Book of Xia*, *The Book of Zhou* and *The Book of Shang*. But the books were disorganized and unknown to most people until Confucius collected and edited them. To assist people to learn from history, he revised and edited these political documents into what later generations called *Collection of Ancient Texts*. It included 50 essays and later developed into 100 essays with forewords before each record ranging chronologically from Yao and Shun to Mu, king of Qi in Spring and Autumn period. By the Period of the Warring States, *The Book of Yao*, *Prayers of Gao Tao*, *Remarks of Yu* and some others were added by later scholars. Among them, the completion of *Hong Fan* was a bit complicated. All of them represent Confucius' thought.

In ancient times, the rites were managed by the officials in charge of history while music was managed by a master musician. But rites and music were lost in wars between the states. Confucius' contributions to history lie not just in his collecting and editing of the lost rites but also his polishing of the rites formed in dynasties of Xia, Shang and Zhou. He taught them to his disciples and even practiced them personally, especially during the time after he came back to Lu.

Confucius classified the rites into eight categories: Mourning, sacrifice, archery, provincial examination, come-of-age ceremony, marriage, courtship and appointment. Under each, there were many subcategories. In *The Analects* there was a story about how Confucius taught Ru Bei the rites of mourning. At first, Confucius did not like Ru Bei and once refused to see him by pretending that he was ill. But even a person such as Ru Bei had a chance to learn some rites, not to mention his excellent disciples such as Yan Hui, Zi Lu, Zi Xia, Zi You and Zeng Shen. Lin Fang, one of Confucius' disciples once asked Confucius about the fundamentals of the rites. Confucius appreciated his question by saying that the rites were the most important and fundamental issue. But it was only after his death that all Confucius' knowledge about rites was collected by his followers into "Three Rites," namely, *The Rites of Zhou*, *The Rites of Ceremony* and *The Book of Rites*, which included a detailed record of all kinds of rites and systems of the time. Thanks to Confucius' contributions, people of today can get to know ancient China by understanding the rites.

The Book of Changes is a book about divination. Its content is very profound but dialectical with many superstitious elements. Confucius always attached importance to *The Book of Changes*, and studied it carefully. He had collected and studied "form," "seal," "telling divinatory symbols," "classic Chinese." It was said that *The Story of Changes* was written by him and that it was a record of his thoughts following his careful study of *The Book of Changes*. Confucius read *The Book of Changes* so often that the ox-hide string tying the book of bamboo strips together came loose. Confucius once said, "Given a few more years to study this book, I will be more efficient in my study and fairly free from errors." Confucius' dialectical thoughts show that he had been affected and enlightened by *The Book of Changes*. It was owing to Confucius' contributions that later generations came to eulogize it as Jing, scriptures, or *The Book of Changes*.

Confucius' contributions on collecting ancient books helped preserve China's ancient culture, and it is justified to regard him as a master collector of classics.

Composing *The Spring and Autumn Annals*

In the early years of Western Zhou, the king of Zhou offered feudal lands to his subjects, and a slavery system came into being. King of Zhou was the ruler of the kingdom, and those outstanding officials who had helped him found the kingdom were honored as "the Marquis." Among the ducal states, officials were called senior officials. Below the senior officials were family subjects and commoners. As for slaves owners and nobles, they had many titles such as duke, marquis, earl, and viscount. The hierarchical system in Zhou Dynasty and the ducal states was so strict that nobody was permitted to bypass or change it. But in the Spring and Autumn Period, with the development of economy, private land ownership was gradually replacing public land ownership and the old system of rites had crumbled, too, in politics. In the early years of Spring and Autumn Period, Duke Huan of Qi united the whole country and then, Duke Wen of Jin forced the king to help him control the various marquises and later, he became a ruler. Duke Mu of Qin in the west came to seize power from the east. The State of Chu, which was ruled by an earl, also came to seek power in central China. The states of Wu and Yue, as ever regarded as inferior foreigners, prospered in the late years of Spring and Autumn Period. At the time, rites and music had crumbled, various marquis struggled for power; senior officials competed for power among the various states, officials killed kings and sons killed fathers — the hierarchy was broken. Under such circumstances, Confucius was determined once he became engaged in politics to make every endeavor to bring back the best time of Western Zhou. This aspiration remained heavy in his heart, and he couldn't forget it for a moment even as he was forced for political reasons to other states. But with the development of society, his idea had become obsolete. Still, Confucius would not give up. He ran schools to foster his followers. Compiling *The Spring and Autumn Annals* was one of the measures to carry out his plan.

To Confucius, the early years of Western Zhou was the best time, therefore it became his criteria for the change of the society of his day. But, finally, he never fulfilled his ideal. He said regretfully in his later years, "How ashamed I feel to see my followers!" To educate his followers to tell right from wrong, Confucius set out to compile the first chronological history of China, *The Spring and Autumn Annals*.

In ancient times, the history of each state was written on specially made bamboo slips. Such historical records are called the Spring and Autumn Annals in the State of Lu. Confucius collected all scattered historical records into a systematic history. The accounts begin from 722 BC (the beginning year of Duke Yin of Lu) and end in 481 BC (the 14th year in the reign of Duke Ai of Lu), covering a span of more than 240 years of history in the early years of Eastern Zhou. Though the historical statements are concise — no more than 40 words for one historical event, in some parts only one word — and though the content is disconnected, it leaves us many historical records.

The Spring and Autumn Annals was the embodiment of Confucius' views. He strongly opposed those who struggled for power and disrespected superiors and started rebellion. He especially opposed the phenomenon of a son's killing his father and/or subjects' killing their rulers, as was best shown by his rectification of names: Duke Wen of Jin had forced the king of Zhou to Heyang to attend his meeting of sovereigns. When recording this period of history, Confucius wrote, "King hunted in Heyang." By deliberately concealing the fact that the king of Zhou was compelled to attend the meeting, Confucius was trying to safeguard the prestige of the king of Zhou. In the late years of the Spring and Autumn Period, one state after another became dominant in central China. The states of Wu and Chu declared themselves as leading powers. But in *The Spring and Autumn Annals*, Confucius called the states according to their official names in the early years of the Zhou Dynasty. For instance, he called the leaders of Chu, earl; Qi and Jin, marquis; Song, the weakest state, duke. No doubt, these statements were inconsistent with the facts, but what Confucius wanted to do was to make a clear distinction between right and wrong by writing the history in view of the standard in the early years of Western Zhou.

In 481 BC (the 14th year in the reign of Duke Ai of Lu), Ju Shang, a cart driver who served Shu Sun Shi, caught a peculiar animal and sent it to Confucius to ask him to identify it. Seeing the animal, Confucius cried out in wonder, "It's a unicorn. Its appearance is an auspicious sign, and it only appears in the reign of a kind king. But where is the kind king?" As Confucius was pondering over the matter, the unicorn died suddenly. Confucius thought this a bad omen and gave a sigh, saying: "What can I do now?" He then stopped writing *The Spring and Autumn Annals*.

The Spring and Autumn Annals, the written history of Lu, has the following characteristics. One is that it values truth. Confucius respected factual historical materials. He said he knew more rites of the Xia and Yin dynasties but little about Qi and Song, for there were less written documents. "If I am given enough materials, I could work them out." The second is that Confucius despised those who concocted history because they had little knowledge about it. He asked himself to listen more and see more. He wrote with great prudence, so as to minimize possible mistakes. The third is that Confucius paid much attention to writing more about current history than he did about ancient times because he thought comments on ancient events and figures should serve contemporary politics. In addition, the language in the book is logical and well-knitted with words selected carefully.

As the first chronological history of China, *The Spring and Autumn Annals* recorded events according to the order of year, month and day, which was helpful for systematic understanding of their inter-relations. *The Annals* set an example for other historical books as a book that serves the political purpose of a class. It was the first history book independently edited by an individual in China. *The Spring and Autumn Annals* put emphasis on the current history and society though it recorded ancient events, which enlightened the followers of Confucius. Furthermore, besides relating something about politics and economy, it conveyed something concerning natural science, especially ancient astronomy, which provided us many valuable materials. Its records on comets and solar eclipse were reliable in science. But sometimes, its records appeared to be too simple, abstract and general, and some records expressed strong fatalism and orthodox ideas. Confucius devoted much effort to editing *The Spring and Autumn Annals*. He said that he used to accept others' opinions in writing, but this time he refused to absorb others' ideas in editing. Even Zi Xia, his favorite and talented disciple, couldn't change a single word. Therefore, Confucius wrote the book completely according to his own ideas. He said, "If I was remembered by later generations, it would be because of *The Spring and Autumn Annals* and if I was blamed, it was *The Spring and Autumn Annals* too." This shows that Confucius placed all his political views into the book.

Mourning over His Disciple's Death

In his late years, Confucius experienced a series of blows with the deaths of his disciples and family members. His wife, Bing Guan Shi, a native of the State of Song, married Confucius when he was 19 years old. Kind and gentle, she stayed at home to support her husband. She gave birth to one son, Kong Li, and one daughter, who later married Gongye Chang, one of Confucius' disciples. For many years after their marriage, life was hard for the couple, but Bing Guan Shi dedicated herself to running the household so that Confucius could have more energy for studying. By the time Confucius took to politics in Lu and their living conditions had improved, Bing Guan Shi still remained at home to educate her children. At the age of 56, Confucius failed in politics in the State of Lu and turned to search for a post in other states; Bing Guan Shi backed his endeavors. Just one year before his returning to Lu, she died of illness in her home. At this news, Confucius was devastated, especially when thinking of what she had done for him, her care and her bravery in the face of poverty. Lonely as he was, Confucius still wanted to complete his unfinished undertaking with his son and daughter on his side. But unfortunately, Kong Li suddenly died.

Kong Li was born when Confucius was at the age of 20. Duke Zhao of Lu celebrated the birth by sending a carp to Confucius, who thought it such a great honor that he named his son "Li" (Carp in Chinese) and styled him "Buo Yu". Admittedly, Confucius had hoped his son would have a meteoric rise and bring fame and honor to his ancestors like the small carp that jumped over a fence and became a dragon in Chinese fairy tales. Kong Li was respectful, submissive and obedient to Confucius. Confucius devoted himself to politics and educating his disciples but spared little time to educate Kong Li and never tried to seek any post for him. Kong Li never asked for anything for the sake of preserving his father's reputation. So at the time of his death, he was still an ordinary civilian. Kong Li took the burden of supporting the family when Confucius was away. When he was 50 years old, Kong Li fell severely ill and soon died of exhaustion. It was a great blow to the 70-year-old Confucius. He buried Kong Li in a coffin without an outer coffin according to the standard for a common civilian. It seems that misfortunes never come singly and one year after Kong Li's death, Confucius' disciple, the 41-year-old Yan Hui died, too.

Clever and fond of learning, Yan Hui was Confucius' favorite disciple. He had a deep understanding of Confucius' doctrine and belief. A handful of rice to eat, a cupful of water to drink, living in a humble dwelling — others might have found it unendurably depressing, but to Yan Hui, it made no difference at all. He followed Confucius in traveling around the various states and was always a faithful companion for him. Confucius always was reluctant to pay a compliment regarding the humanity of anyone, but with the exception of Yan Hui. Though Yan Hui was poor, he cherished a great aspiration for governing the nation with virtue and serving the people. Owing to the poverty of his family and hard work in his studies, Yan Hui suffered bad health. At 29, he had white hair, and at 41 he died.

At the news, Confucius was in great distress and shouted: "It's the will of heaven!"

Withered Away the Sage

The series of blows Confucius suffered — the death of his son, wife and his favorite disciple — took their toll, and in his late years Confucius became weaker and weaker. He was dissatisfied with many affairs such as Ji Sun Shi's new system of field taxation in Lu and Chen Heng murdering his sovereign in the State of Qi.

Chen Heng, a nobleman of the State of Chen, who had fled to Qi (and changed his name to Tian Shi) and been in power for eight generations, bought popular support by all means to expand his power. In 481 BC, Chen Heng (whose name had been changed to Tian Cheng Zi), who was the top executive officer in Qi, killed his sovereign and seized the highest power of Qi. This event was just a prelude to the carving up of Jin by the families of Han, Zhao and Wei and the first action made by the new and developing landlord class to seize the power of the slave owners and nobles. The State of Qi established by Tian Shi was the first local feudal power in China.

At the news of Chen Heng's having seized

power, Confucius, 71 at the time, fasted and bathed to prepare for a visit to the Duke Ai of Lu to ask him to fight against Chen Heng. But Duke Ai of Lu assigned the mission to the "Three Families," i.e. the family of Meng, Shu and Ji. The three families and Chen Heng were all of new and developing strength, so naturally they were reluctant to fight against Chen Heng. But Confucius had thought that more than half of the people in Qi would oppose Chen Heng, for he had killed their ruler. With the support of Lu, wasn't it certain that Chen would be driven off the throne? Confucius' judgment was groundless in his thinking that there ought to have been quite a number of people like him concerned with safeguarding the old system.

Confucius' proposal of fighting against the treacherous Chen was declined. The following year, Zifu Jingbo and Zi Gong were sent officially to Qi to express their wishes to be on good terms with Qi. This, no doubt, was a great blow to Confucius, the guard of the old system.

In his last two years, Confucius was seriously ill. The disappointments in politics, poor life, and loneliness after the death of his wife, son and disciple had caused him great pain. Though Zi Gong, Zi Xia and Zeng Shen came to visit him, this did not relieve his sadness. Trapped in failure and unable to find a way out, Confucius became more nostalgic for ancient times. In his dreams, he kept dreaming of the Duke of Zhou and talking with him about the rites of flourishing Western Zhou and sharing with him the irritating reality. But as time went by and his mind became more and more insensible and disordered, the Duke of Zhou stopped appearing in his dreams. Thus, Confucius had to give a long sigh, and he became more and more pessimistic.

One night, Confucius had a dream that left him feeling so uneasy that he managed to get up before dawn and — supported by his walking stick — leaned against the door. When Zi Gong came to see him, Confucius said to him, "Why are you so late to see me?" And then he recited a poem:

Fallen Mount Tai!

Collapsed the great beam!

Withered away the great sage!

At this, Zi Gong said, "If Mount Tai has fallen, how can people survive? If the beam has collapsed, how can the house stand and if the sage has withered away, who can lead us? You must be sick." With these words, he supported Confucius back inside the house.

Back in bed, Confucius told Zi Gong about his dream in which he was together with his ancestors. After that, he became more and more ill, and soon he died in 479 BC (in the 16th year of the reign of Duke Ai of Lu), on February 11, in the Chinese lunar calendar. Confucius was buried near the bank of the Sishui River, more than one mile north of

Lu City. His disciples built an elliptical grave. Many disciples who came to mourn brought with them saplings to plant around the grave. Eventually they grew into a forest and called by later generations "forest of Confucius." The place where Confucius' disciples lived while guarding the grave for three years was called "Kong Li" (Confucius' home). Through years of development, the "forest of Confucius" covers an area of more than one square kilometer.

Confucius has been loyal to his sovereign. After Confucius' death, Duke Ai of Lu missed him very much, writing in his mourning article: "How cruel is heaven! You don't even leave me such an old man of high noble character and prestige. I am so lonely that I feel as if I were ill. Confucius, whom should I consult with after your death?"

Confucius had stated that "I preach but I don't write anything." Throughout his life, except for collating some classics, he seldom wrote anything. Later his remarks were collected by his disciples and compiled, into *The Analects*, which is famous for its profound philosophic theories, penetrating analysis and concise statement. Some comments were to the point in simple sentences, some vivid and specific and some deep in thought. It has become a well known classic of the pre-Qin period and important material for studying Confucius' thoughts.

After his death, Confucius was honored with

numerous posthumous titles by emperors in different dynasties such as "Supreme Sage and Foremost Teacher," "Great Perfect Sage, Most Holy Culture Spreading King," "A Great Sage in this Fateful World, and an Ideal Teacher for Myriads of Years" to mention just a few. He has been the greatest ancient Chinese sage for more than 2,000 years. Confucianism, created by and named after Confucius, has been the most important part of Chinese traditional culture after so many years of inheritance, innovation and development. When Emperor Qian Long went on a pilgrimage to Qufu in the thirteenth year of his reign (in 1748), he wrote a poem on that occasion, entitled "A Poem Composed Drunk When Paying Homage at Confucius' Mausoleum." The poem says:

"Your teaching will long benefit the generations.
Mount Tai will stand as witness.
And this is true."

Appendix: Chronicle of Events in the Life of Confucius

551 BC, i.e., in the 22nd year in the reign of Duke Xiang of Lu: Confucius was born in Zouyi, Changping, in the State of Lu. His father, Shu Liangge, was a senior official of Zouyi; his mother was Yan Zhengzai.

549 BC, in the 24th year in the reign of Duke Xiang of Lu: When Confucius was three years old, his father died and was buried at Fang Mountain, east of the capital of Lu. Soon after, his mother moved with her son to Queli in the capital of Lu.

546 BC, in the 27th year in the reign of Duke Xiang of Lu: When Confucius was six years old, he practiced "rites" for the first time while playing with his friends.

537 BC, in the 5th year in the reign of Duke Zhao of Lu: When Confucius was 15 years old, he said to himself, "I am fifteen. I must begin to learn a career."

535 BC, in the 7th year in the reign of Duke Zhao of Lu: When Confucius was 17 years old, his mother died. She was buried with his father. Con-

fucius tried to take part in the banquet held by Ji Sun Shi, but failed.

533 BC, in the 9th year in the reign of Duke Zhao of Lu: When Confucius was 19 years old, he married Bing Guan Shi from the State of Song.

532 BC, in the 10th year in the reign of Duke Zhao of Lu: When Confucius was 20 years old, he was appointed to take charge of first the farmland and later the storehouse of Ji Sun Shi. His son was born. Since Duke Zhao of Lu had a carp sent to him, he named his son Li (meaning carp) and Bo Yu (meaning fish) as his style name.

525 BC, in the 17th year in the reign of Duke Zhao of Lu: When Confucius was 27 years old, Tan Zi came to Lu. Confucius learned rites from him. At the same time, Confucius learned how to play the zither from Shi Xiang.

522 BC, in the 20th year in the reign of Duke Zhao of Lu: When Confucius was 30 years old, he told himself that it was the age to be well established in his career, so he started a school. He enrolled students such as Yan Lu, Zeng Dian and Zhong You. Zi Chan, a senior official from the State of Zheng, who was highly regarded by Confucius died.

518 BC, in the 24th year in the reign of Duke Zhao of Lu: When Confucius was 34 years old, he enrolled Meng Yizi and Nangong Jingshu as his students, and he went to Luoyi to learn rites from

Lao Zi. He visited Ming Hall and Li Mu Temple.

517 BC, in the 25th year in the reign of Duke Zhao of Lu: When Confucius was 35 years old, Duke Zhao of Lu was driven out of Lu by Ji Shi because of an incident at a cockfight. Confucius went to the State of Qi and called on Duke Jing of Qi via Gao Zhaozi.

516 BC, in the 26th year in the reign of Duke Zhao of Lu: When Confucius was 36 years old, Confucius stayed in Qi and discussed music with Qi Tai Shi. He listened to Shao Music. Confucius discussed politics with Duke Jing who intended to grant the land of Nixi to Confucius.

515 BC, in the 27th year in the reign of Duke Zhao of Lu: When Confucius was 37 years old, Yan Ying, a senior official of Qi, and other officials stopped Duke Jing of Qi from granting land to Confucius. Confucius left Qi and went back to Lu.

510 BC, in the 32nd year in the reign of Duke Zhao of Lu: When Confucius was 41 years old, Duke Zhao of Lu died in Qianhou, State of Jin. His death made Confucius dissatisfied with Ji Sun Shi.

501 BC, in the 9th year in the reign of Duke Ding of Lu: When Confucius was 51 years old, he was appointed the governor of Zhongdu.

500 BC, in the 10th year in the reign of Duke Ding of Lu: When Confucius was 52 years old, he took the post of Minister of Works of Lu, and was

then promoted to be the Great Minister of Justice. He acted as regent premier when Lu and Qi had a meeting at Jiagu.

498 BC, in the 12th year in the reign of Duke Ding of Lu: When Confucius was 54 years old, he abandoned the three smaller capitals in order to weaken the power of the senior officials. He led his army and succeeded in his attacks on the city of Hou and city of Fei, but failed at the city of Cheng.

497 BC, in the 13th year in the reign of Duke Ding of Lu: When Confucius was 55 years old, the senior officials of Qi — fearing a stronger State of Lu because of Confucius' presence there — had some dancing girls and singers sent to the Lord of Lu to divert him from state affairs. Confucius was so angry at the Lord of Lu's indulgences as to leave Lu for the State of Wei. On his way, he was entrapped in Kuang and Pu. After that, he went back to Wei.

496 BC, in the 14th year in the reign of Duke Ding of Lu: When Confucius was 56 years old, he stayed in Wei and met Nan Zi. He toured with Duke Ling of Wei.

493 BC, in the 2nd year in the reign of Duke Ai of Lu: When Confucius was 59 years old, an internal disturbance broke out in Wei. When asked by the Duke Ling of Wei for advice, Confucius gave him no reply. After that, Confucius planned to cross the Yellow River to go to the State of Jin, but failed.

492 BC, in the 3rd year in the reign of Duke Ai of Lu: When Confucius was 60 years old, he left Wei for Chen. On his way, he passed through the states of Cao, Song and Zheng.

489 BC, in the 6th year in the reign of Duke Ai of Lu: When Confucius was 63 years old, he left Chen for Cai. On the way, he and his followers were besieged by enemy troops and had nothing to eat, but he played music and kept composure. After getting out of the siege, he went to the State of Chu. There, Chu Zhao Wang (the Duke) planned to grant him the land of Shushe, but failed because of the strong opposition of some senior officials of the state.

485 BC, in the 10th year in the reign of Duke Ai of Lu When Confucius was 67 years old, his wife died while he was staying in Wei.

484 BC, in the 11th year in the reign of Duke Ai of Lu: When Confucius was 68 years old, Ji Huanzi invited him back to Lu where Confucius compiled books of poems and revised books of rites and music, wrote *The Spring and Autumn Annals*. He taught more than 3,000 students, among whom, over seventy were masters of "six arts".

483 BC, in the 12th year in the reign of Duke Ai of Lu: When Confucius was 69 years old, Kong Li, son of Confucius, died.

482 BC, in the 13th year in the reign of Duke Ai of Lu: When Confucius was 70 years old, he told

himself "to do what he liked at seventy but within its scale". He studied the *Book of Changes* (*I-Ching*) very diligently. Yan Hui, one of his best students, died.

481 BC, in the 14th year in the reign of Duke Ai of Lu: When Confucius was 71 years old, he bagged a kylin (a Chinese unicorn) when hunting in the west in the springtime. He finished *The Spring and Autumn Annals*. Chen Heng, a senior official of the State of Qi, killed his Duke. Confucius asked the Duke of Lu to attack him but was rejected.

480 BC, in the 15th year in the reign of Duke Ai of Lu: When Confucius was 72 years old, Zi Lu, one of his best students, was killed in a riot in the State of Wei.

479 BC, in the 16th year in the reign of Duke Ai of Lu: When Confucius was 73 years old, he died and was buried at Sishang, north of the capital of Lu (the present-day Qufu, Shandong Province).

图书在版编目（CIP）数据

孔子的故事/骆承烈著.
—北京：外文出版社，2002.6
ISBN 7-119-03071-x

I.孔…II.骆…III.孔丘（前551—前479）-生平事迹-英文
IV.B222.25

中国版本图书馆 CIP 数据核字（2002）第 039778 号

英文主译　阿拉坦
英文翻译　李永贵　王新　庞丽霞
责任编辑　吴灿飞　贾先锋
封面设计　王　志
插图绘制　李士伋
印刷监制　冯　浩

外文出版社网址：
http://www.flp.com.cn
外文出版社电子信箱：
info@flp.com.cn
sales@flp.com.cn

孔子的故事
骆承烈著
*
©外文出版社
外文出版社出版
（中国北京百万庄大街 24 号）
邮政编码　100037
春雷印刷厂印刷
中国国际图书贸易总公司发行
（中国北京车公庄西路 35 号）
北京邮政信箱第 399 号　邮政编码　100044
2004 年(36 开)第 1 版
2004 年第 1 版第 1 次印刷
（英）
ISBN 7-119-03071-x/I.723(外)
03600(平)
10-E-3487P